The Enochian Legacy

The Alien/UFO Enigma
'Angels Of Light
or
Angels Of Darkness'

An insight into the sacred writings of Enoch, whose revelations concerning the existence of Angels in the distant past, compares strongly with the modern worldwide Alien & UFO experience.

PAUL C. ABEL

ANGELS OF LIGHT - ANGELS OF DARKNESS

A Tree of Heaven Publication

© Copyright 2003

THE ENOCHIAN LEGACY, 'Angels of Light - Angels of Darkness' by Paul C. Abel. THE AUTHOR asserts his Moral & Spiritual Rights to the ownership and association of this work. No portion of this book may be reproduced or copied in any form, or held in a retrieval system, or produced in any other binding or form without the express permission of the Author of this work.

ISBN: 0-9546542-0-X

Printed by:
ProPrint
Riverside Cottages
Old Great North Road
Stibbington
Cambs. PE8 6LR

Front cover design
Extract from *"Fifty Years of UFOs:*
From Distant Sightings to Close Encounters'
By John & Ann Spencer

Original design by: The Image Bank (1997)

Angels of Light - Angels of Darkness

I dedicate this work to:

My Wife Mala, for her unfailing love, endearment, personal suffering, strength and courage, who, not always understanding why, supported me just the same.

And to my daughter Nina for her continual inspiration, willingness to listen, encouragement and support in making this work possible.

Also to my brother Edwin, for the many hours of biblical debate as well as his unfailing recognition concerning some of the issues raised in this book and also to my Father, for whom nothing is certain but the truth.

ACKNOWLEDGEMENTS

Firstly, I would like to thank Enoch for his words of wisdom and truth regarding the existence of Angels and whose work has spanned the corridors of time to grasp my attention.

Secondly, I would like to thank the Reverend M. R. James of King's College, Cambridge, for discovering the Enochian fragments (hidden away in The British Museum), as well as the author R. H. Charles (1855 - 1931), for his translation of the Aramaic/Hebrew text of the book of Enoch, into English.

I would also like to thank both ancient, and modern writers, on the subject of Ufology, the Paranormal etc., for the many hours of thought provoking and challenging reading materials and researches, that have helped to clarify my own personal quest for understanding, knowledge, and above all, truth, concerning the Alien & UFO enigma.

Another source of inspiration to which I am greatly indebted is that of the Holy Bible. The quotes and scriptural references used are taken from the King James Version of the Bible with the exception of those references quoted from the Book of Enoch all other references are contained in the Bibliography.

Finally, I would like to thank the authors listed in the Bibliography for their special interest in the subject of Ufology. In particular, I thank them for taking the trouble to actually listen to all of us who have experienced personal encounters with the unknown and to say that we are promised one day that: "We shall know the Truth and the Truth shall set us free". May that day come sooner rather than later.

CONTENTS

CHAPTERS	Page No:
Introduction	i – vi
Astronomical Secrets	1
The Fall of the Angels & The Demise of Mankind	17
A Brief Encounter with the Unknown	27
Mount Hermon by Mutual Imprecation	33
The Mystery of the Harrier Jump Jet	39
The Things Mankind Has Learned To Do	43
The Doorway to Other Dimensions	49
Vision of a Brilliant White Light over Stoney Cross	59
Opening of the Windows in Heaven	65
A vision of a Heavenly Chariot	71
The Trouble with Angels	77
My Quest for an answer to some of the Enigmas	81
Disillusionment and World change	89
Angels of Light	97
Further Strange Encounters	105
Bibliography	113

THE ENOCHIAN LEGACY

Angel Definition

Extract from the Readers Digest, UNIVERSAL DICTIONARY, 1987.

1. ANGEL. Noun. 1. Theology.
A). An Immortal, Spiritual Being attendant upon God. An Angel is conventionally represented as a "Winged" being of human form.

B). In Medieval Angelology, an Angel is one of nine orders of spiritual beings (listed from the highest in rank to the lowest): Seraphim, Cherubim, Thrones, Dominions or Dominations, Virtues, Powers and Principalities, Archangels and Angels.

2. A Guardian Spirit.

Enoch & the Archangel Michael

INTRODUCTION

In the distant shadows of the antediluvian age, (circa 22,071 BC), there lived a man called Enoch. As a preacher of righteousness, Enoch tells an incredible story concerning the existence of Angels and their involvement in the fall of mankind. He believes that his account of their existence is something that the whole world should know about. Through his writings, Enoch reveals how mankind has been duped into believing that the human race is exclusively to blame for the fall of man and more importantly, his discoveries uncover information relating to *'the Judgement'*, as well as the future destiny of mankind.

Through his evidence, Enoch reveals that a great deception had unfolded around him and that the perpetrators of this fraudulent deception were none other than a group of alien beings known as 'the Watchers'. From his records, it appears that these watchers have originated from some as yet, unknown place in the universe.

Furthermore, the evidence concerning the existence of these alien beings and their purpose for being here on Earth, leads Enoch to the knowledge that this deception was the first major phase of a cunning master plan designed by the watchers, intended to bring about the detriment of all God's creation, (including mankind), if the perpetrators could not effectively be brought to justice.

Having made this discovery, Enoch also learned that on a previous occasion one of these watchers, a 'serpent being' named Gadreel, had visited the Earth in the distant past during the lifetime of Adam and Eve, (circa 22,932 BC), and this visit was apparently to establish the original devices for the demise of mankind. According to Enoch, it was Eve who was originally beguiled by this serpent mentor at that time.

Enoch concludes his discoveries with further knowledge that, in the youthful days of his father Jared, a group of similar serpent-like alien beings from among the watchers, called 'The Satans', had been visiting the Earth in large numbers. Enoch informs us that they originally descended near the summit of mount Hermon in the Antillibinus Mountain region north of modern Israel, and that their apparent purpose for this second encounter was the watcher's attraction to human women, as implied in the book of Genesis (Ch6 v 1-7).

Enoch's desire for the truth concerning these past encounters brings about his own personal encounter with the same group of alien beings, some of whom had apparently been caught and placed in 'Abel's jail'. According to Enoch, their captors placed the watchers in this jail until they could find a way to deal justly with them for their crimes against humanity. This appears to be a clear indication that these space beings are not entirely infallible despite their high status, (a similar suggestion of fallibility also appears to be presented by the 'Roswell Incident' of 1947 and the 'Socorro Incident' a year later, in which it is alleged, that similar alien beings called 'Greys' were also captured).

During his second encounter with the captured aliens, the watchers attempt to enlist the support of Enoch by asking him to represent them in putting forward a case for their defence to the living God, the Judge of the whole world, the Lord of Spirits, The God of Heaven and Earth, and because of the level of his involvement with the aliens, Enoch soon came face to face with four other powerful alien beings who revealed themselves as 'Archangels'. Apparently, these beings were also descended from among the watchers on high. These four alien beings reveal to Enoch that they were sent from God, the 'Lord of Spirits', to bring the 'fallen angels' to a judgement in which, "they are to carry out a death sentence against all those unjust perpetrators of the kingdom of God" (Cited in: Charles 1997, page 34). The reason the Archangels give for this action is "that as angels, these particular beings have transgressed their holy estate" (Jude, verses 5 - 16), for the ubiquitous favour of women under which cause, they have become the prime suspects of an evil paradox that affects not just the present, but also the future of mankind. According to Enoch, this action has resulted in the setting of an eternal judgement upon themselves as well as the human race because of their unearthly union with human women, which God had expressly forbidden. During this process, Enoch is made aware of their individual identities whilst at the same time being instructed by them in the secrets of the universe. This deeper knowledge that Enoch gained from his close encounters with the Archangels,

Michael, Raphael, Phanuel and Uriel, enlightens Enoch to the truth that the history of mankind will culminate in a second and final judgement of the world, involving both the living and the dead, by the Lord of spirits. Furthermore, he reveals that this judgement will also be followed by a special judgement against the angels themselves and in particular, those who have betrayed the Living God through evil indulgences. Because of his newfound relationship with the Archangels, Enoch was chosen to write down all the secrets that they had shown to him concerning the watchers and their demise and in particular, he was instructed to 'observe' and 'record' everything that he learned for the posterity of mankind that would develop after the flood. This record was apparently made in the hope that mankind would eventually know the truth about Alien existence and the reasons that lay behind man's own fate. The Archangels hoped that the statute of judgement placed upon everything on Earth and in Heaven, would cause mankind to seek God's forgiveness for the part that humanity has played in allowing sin to enter God's creation, but even to this day, many still refuse to recognise or accept this important aspect of God's work. However, *'The Enochian Legacy, Angels of Light or Angels of Darkness'* is not just about Enoch's encounters with strange angelic, alien beings from space, but is also about the modern worldwide UFO & Alien enigma that currently exists, because since 1947, there has been countless sightings similar in nature to that recorded by Enoch, also involving strange, luminous aerial objects, that we now call UFO's. Moreover, it is a matter of public record since 1947, that UFO's have been increasingly sighted, along with the stories of abductions of humans, (involving mostly women and children), as well as other strange phenomenon such as Crop Circle Formations, unexplained animal mutilations and the more recent sightings of alien beasts.

Despite these bizarre occurrences, world Governments continue to deny that anything strange is taking place around the world, but still the reports are consistently being made. Credible witnesses from all occupations are increasingly reporting UFO sightings. These include the armed forces, pilots, police officers, doctors and scientists as well as thousands of ordinary people, many of whom are increasingly affected by UFO encounters, and long for an official explanation about the occurrences of this strange phenomenon.

The book of Enoch is emphatic about his descriptions concerning the existence of alien beings and the fact that he quotes their names and records their numerous skills, suggests that these beings should be taken literally. If what Enoch suggests is a true record of these beings from space, then it must equally be a true record about the 'First Judgement' and 'the Flood', evidence of which, may lie under the oceans and coastal regions and dating back to approximately 22,930 years. If this is true, then we must without a doubt, take into account, that Enoch's record concerning the 'Final Judgement' of mankind must also be a true account. The question is this however, is mankind really prepared for the truth about the existence of Angels or Aliens as revealed by Enoch? I very much doubt it. Can we really afford to ignore the weight of evidence that Enoch has presented for us today concerning the existence of UFO's, Crop Circles and Aliens? What is more, should we continue to close our eyes to the current world changes taking place in our world today that also reflect the prophetic evidence revealed by Enoch, and which, if true, is actually happening in our time?

The Bible says that: "As in the days of Noah so shall it be in the days when the Son of Man comes!" (Cited in: Luke 17 v 26-30). One of the main features of this biblical statement is an apparent increase in 'hedonism' that was partially responsible for the earlier Angel encounters and which, had strong links to *'the pleasure principle'* and solar cult worship that was being invoked at that time along with the worship of 'other gods'. According to Enoch, this same aspect of human activity is increasingly linked to similar destructive weather systems including Global Warming and floods that we see today, and these are just some of those major signs of the 'days of Noah', can we truly afford to ignore this?

Is it true also, that the American government is in contact with a group of alien beings, commonly called 'the Greys', who are believed to be living under the sea just off Mount Aricebo, and who, apparently, are frequently seen as visitors to our skies? Is it true also, that these 'Greys' are the ones currently responsible for the spate of abductions on record today? Just how does one explain the frequency of evidence regarding UFO encounters that are reported?

The truth concerning alien existence, is clearly out there for all of us to recognise, but unfortunately, the evidence of alien existence has been deliberately presented to us in the form of a 'crock of gold', such as the film, *"Close Encounters of the Third Kind"* for example, a form of propaganda apparently placed openly at our doorsteps, supposedly by governmental intervention, (according to some researchers), via the media, and which, the debunker of the UFO abduction phenomenon and UFO's in general, is said to have deliberately tampered with to promote uncertainty and confusion as part of a common denial attempt. The media is fully aware that the problem with the majority of people worldwide is that they often fail to recognise what is right in front of their faces, and this factor enables the media to make the truth less credible. Furthermore, the mass media's realisation for using such unique approaches enables them to make full use of these powerful mediums such as Hollywood Movies or Television propaganda to influence public opinion into a false sense of security. For example, the use of these visual techniques serve as a clever psychological instrument through which, Cinema, Television or Video technology can be used as a powerful subliminal medium for "searing the human conscience with a hot iron", (Cited in: The Bible, 1 Timothy 4 v 2). This may well be a factor also for the increase in violence already being realised in modern society and which is a major concern for us all. It is for this reason too, that it becomes impossible for us to accept the truth of any subject easily, without fear of it. For with these same mediums, we are ultimately encouraged into a state of unbelief where we eventually become "mockers of the truth" (Cited in: Jude 1 v 1-16 & 18-19).

Furthermore, the public's uncertainty about the future of our world means that years of skilled manipulation by these credible forces also enables them to establish their purposes which lay behind the secret history of our social development and which may include Alien intelligences.

This book attempts to show a conjunction with Enoch's experiences during the antediluvian period, the modern UFO enigma, and the author, who has cached his own personal encounters and observations around Enoch's writings in an attempt to inform the reader about the past and future demise of mankind. I offer my own belief that Aliens have visited the planet Earth for thousands of years and are consistently involved in the evolutionary processes affecting mankind, even to this day.

'The Enochian Legacy, Angels of Light or Angels of darkness', is a vehicle that seeks to demonstrate juxtaposition outlined by the contents of the fragments of Enoch's writings with that of my own personal experiences about alien existence. However, it is entirely up to the reader to draw his or her own conclusions as to the reality of these matters, for in the end only you can decide whether or not there is truth in these connections with the book of Enoch and the modern wave of UFO stories.

Paul Abel, 2003

CHAPTER ONE

Astronomical Secrets

"And there mine eyes saw the secrets of the lightning and of the thunder, and the secrets of the wind... As well as the secrets of the cloud and dew and the place from whence they proceed, and of the Sun and the Moon, the hail, and the mist.

I saw their comings and goings and their glorious return, and how they keep faith with one another..."

"And I asked the Angel who went with me who showed me what was hidden: 'What are these?'" (Cited in: Charles 1997, page 62)

Jesus said: "What I tell you in the darkness, speak ye in the light; and what ye hear in the ear, proclaim upon the rooftops" (Cited in: Matthew 10 v 27).

"I will utter things that have been kept secret from the foundation of the world" (Cited in: Matthew 13 v 35 & Mark 4 v 22).

It has been reported that unknown intelligences are visiting the Earth. The discovery of the existence of 'extraterrestrial beings', has been acknowledged recently by the media, and is now viewed as the inevitable confirmation, that we are truly not alone in this universe after all. The thousands of witnesses to alien phenomenon and the abduction experience are just too overwhelming for us to continue to dismiss the UFO & Alien enigma, as a figment of pure imagination, or simply a shift in human consciousness.

Since the advent of the Papal System, dominant church leaders have consistently played down the existence of 'otherworldly forces' in a long-term conspiracy against the human race. The Church is said to be responsible for attempting to hide the truth that lies behind our existence and control the world in which we live.

The world may not be aware that the Enochian Fragments, The Bible, The Koran as well as many other ancient documents like the

Mahabaratha, for example, and many Hindu Vedic writings, speak of the existence of Alien Beings, Angels or 'Watchers' as descending from heaven, as beings from another dimension or otherworldly existence. There is no doubt, that the most compelling of evidence ever recorded about alien existence, can be found within the written fragments of the book of Enoch.

Throughout the history of the world, mankind has developed incredible skills. Among these skills is the ability to observe everything that surrounds our existence and one of the most important reasons for this particular development, has been the need to understand the mysteries of life itself, but more importantly than this, is whether or not we are alone in this universe. Who we are, and how we came to exist on this planet that we call 'Earth', has been a major pre-requisite to our understanding of the world in which we live and our observations of it.

Historically, mankind owes a considerable debt to those many inspired individuals from our past whose wisdom has been acquired through their studies of our Earthly environment and the universe in general, including the sun, moon, stars, and the planets and how these might be formed. These great men are said to have recorded their observations with reasonable accuracy by utilising the tools available to them in their time. In fact, the earliest recorded attempts to study the world and its surroundings scientifically, dates back to ancient Egypt and Babylon.

Historical recognition has also been accorded to a number of great observers whose sciences have been accepted by the media in general and include men such as: Eratosthenes of Cyrene, Thales of Miletus, Pythagoras of Greece, Euclid of Alexandria and Aristotle the Greek, to name but a few. However, there are many great men of understanding and knowledge from the pages of history that the world knows very little of, and the recorded observations of these men, have been lost to antiquity, dating back to the distant recesses of time, to the antediluvian period.

Prior to the Antediluvian age, which I believe to be during *'The Upper Palaeolithic' and 'Epi-Palaeolithic'* periods, circa 25000 BC - 8500 BC, (according to the Times Atlas of The Bible, 1994 edition), during which, there lived a number of wise seers. These men are lesser-known figures, such as Adam, Seth, Enoch and Noah, whose names only appear in the Bible but who have left behind a number of written works containing their observations and personal experiences for the benefit of mankind.

In fact, what the world is unaware of, is that those great men to whom history accords the beginnings of our Earthly sciences to, actually got the basics of their insights and knowledge from the surviving ancient manuscripts written by those men I have named above. These manuscripts, many of which, are surviving copies of original works carried over from the flood by Noah, are in fact earlier established writings of these truly great men like Enoch. Incidentally, writing is considered to have been discovered (circa 4000 BC), and at this time it is considered that there existed three differing writing forms: Cunieform, Hieratic and Pictorial.

In my view however, writing is at least 22,000 years old despite the established view and this is based on evidence linked to the Jewish calendar and that places the origins of writing well within the Antediluvian era. In my opinion also, it is the writings of Enoch, (whose works were re-discovered among the fragments of the Dead Sea scrolls, in the early eighteenth century AD.), that these fragments are among the most important pieces of ancient historical information to have ever been recorded from the Antediluvian era.

The Bible itself, mentions very little about Enoch, except to say that this man walked with God and that his relationship with God was such that He took him. However, The Enochian fragments contain some of the most profound information ever discovered and which, surprisingly enough, covers not only our ancient past, but our present and also the future history and destiny of mankind.

In medieval times, referred to as the 'Dark Ages', man's observations proved misleading and inaccurate. This was largely due to the religious influences of the 'Papal System' that exploited the ignorance and superstition of the masses that existed during this period through the iconography of daemons, witches and faeries etc.

For example, the devil was the subject of universal belief, and this was viewed as a desirable methodology of the times aimed at controlling the way that men thought about their surroundings. These ideas were rigidly based on the particular religious and paranormal experiences that people had with regard to the concept of life in general and their particular belief systems, which they manufactured to rationalise current perceptions at that time.

Author David Ovason alludes to this same point when he writes that it was "the introduction of this spiritual and intellectual myopia called 'Rationalism' that was fast becoming a part of European culture during the rise of the dark ages and during this same period, attempts to link the Earth with stellar influences were rejected as superstitious. Those who worked within secret societies or spiritual communities and who persisted in this way, had to find alternative ways to communicate their virtues" (Cited in: Ovason 1999, page 454).

During the middle ages, human reason had begun to displace faith, and Rationalism began to exceed fundamental Christian principals, forcing a major change upon dogmatic theology, especially within the Roman Church. This particular movement aided the spread of irreligious and indifferentist opinions justifying the movement of the social pendulum towards maintaining the ideologies of Empiricism, Sensualism, and Scepticism through vein philosophies and an upsurge in Materialism. This unsettling of Christian revelation opposed by the tenets of reason led to the rejection of everything in Christianity that flavoured of the supernatural. Instead, the rationalists tended towards Deism and Naturalism which they made quite fashionable but which, are merely a clever disguise for paganism and pantheism. The drive towards Naturalism developed into a system of thought that holds that all phenomena can be explained in terms of natural causes accompanied by natural laws without the added moral or spiritual or supernatural significances placed upon it by Christianity.

It does seem however, that our ability to rationalise everything, is a basic human trait and this trait enables us to cover up supernatural phenomenon or disguise them, or simply deny their existence and even dismiss them altogether. In fact, when we do not have any reasonable or scientific answers for anything we cannot understand, truly reason with, or dislike, then we reduce these phenomenon to something of non-importance, but like it or not, the universe is full of unexplainable phenomenon and strange occurrences, and many of these unexplainable, yet strange happenings are classified by the rationalists as 'natural phenomena' and may even be officially recorded as such. Nevertheless, despite the advancements mankind has made in perfecting our ability to rationalise our existence, unexplainable phenomenon continues to remain. This type of rationalism enables us to avoid subjects pertaining to supernatural occurrences unless, like many people, one happens to encounter such phenomena at a personal level.

In the mainstream of life however, our physical and observable world is fully documented and understood, both in metaphysical and scientific terms. Nevertheless, the most common effect throughout the history of mankind, directly resulting from the influence of unexplained phenomena, appears to be that of 'religious fervour', which is often linked to the 'raising of consciousness', and that seems to accompany such events much like that of the recent 'New Age thinking'. This modern wave of influence appears to have come about because of 'Crop circles' and the numerous recorded 'UFO sightings' and including the more bizarre 'Alien abductions' apparently taking place worldwide since 1945.

With regard to the crop circles phenomenon, Pat Delgado and Colin Andrews, authors of the book *'Circular Evidence' (1989)*, state "that there is a belief that these circles, despite efforts to prove the contrary, are predominantly the work of Supernatural Intelligences". In contrast to this theory the meteorologist, Dr Terrence Meiden believes that Crop Circles "are a peculiar form of downwardly spiralling vortices that predominantly occur on open fields near hills", but his efforts to prove this have been thwarted by the very circles themselves occurring elsewhere, and in constantly changing patterns. Crop Circles became more widely known during the mid 1960's and 1970's when pictograms, and circles with satellite rings, as well as concentric circles, began to appear in fields throughout the world with alarming frequency and thereby proving Dr Meiden wrong in his assumptions.

During this same period a British radio astronomer called, G.S. Hawkins discovered a 3rd, 4th, and 5th dimension reality, which appeared to be incorporated into the geometry of the crop circles. He noted that these dimensions correlated in a musical pitch theme known as 'diatonic ratios' similar to that reported in the field of Geodesics, and which, he says conclusively suggests that many of the circles found in the countryside *are* predominantly the work of 'non-human intelligences'.

In fact, UFO encounters, recently witnessed in increasing numbers in South America and in particular Mexico, as well as other countries of the world, has inspired a rather curious upsurge in the raising of 'Consciousness' throughout the seventies. This may well be due, in part at least, to a deeper desire in the heart and mind of man for the need to believe. Believe that is, not only in his existence, or in himself, but also in the concept of higher beings, or the existence of a creator. Once again it is a fact, from the rationalist point of view, that when we are unable to supply suitably contrived solutions to issues of this nature, or to furnish a satisfactory explanation for many of these disturbing yet fascinating events, those deeply affected by them, may turn to religious belief and practices once more.

It would seem that religion, and not the sciences, offers at the very least, some form of satisfying explanation and possibly a feeling of protection, against that which cannot be rationalised or scientifically understood, such as 'death', for example, for although we can explain the physical aspects of death scientifically, we are as yet, unable to fully provide an explanation or a justification for its occurrence within the human life cycle, except in religious terms. However, the Bible does provide a religious justification for the cause of death by relating this cause to 'original sin' and the fall of man, whilst offering hope in the form of salvation from death, through the personage of the Lord Jesus Christ.

In fact, it has been observed that certain dramatic events, which challenge our mortality throughout the history of mankind, has itself, led to several increases in religious fervour around the globe, and which has perpetuated changes in religion, and also in the moral, political and social structures through which we have developed a deepening association, both in spiritual and secular terms. Indeed, our Industrial efforts have also evolved from our basic need to overcome the fears and doubts that have surrounded us, from the dawn of time.

The centuries of religious and scientific discovery, which are handed down from generation to generation, apparently have its roots in the stars. Certainly, we owe much to those who have passed before us, as each one of us that pass this way is a reflection of the one that has gone before and in this state it would appear that our uniqueness is the result of a fine balance that the universe holds around us.

Consider this point thoroughly! One degree of change in the Earth's rotational path really could spell the end for all life on Earth if it were not for the apparent self-regulating motion of the heavens as a whole, and the stability of the Earth upon which we live and die. One degree of change within the Earth's movement, rotation and orbit through space could place human and animal existence in total jeopardy.

According to the Reverend G. R. Jeffrey, *'The Anthropic Principle'* suggests that there is a range of scientific variables for the existence of life on our planet and that these variables, such as our atmosphere, the relevant distance from the sun, the chemical compositions of Earth's soil and so on, are the pre-requisites we need for life to exist and prosper. If our solar system was anything slightly different, we could never have evolved and if the rotational effect of our planets 24-hour cycle failed to keep pace with Earth's precise ability, then desolation would ensue, (Cited in: Jeffrey, 1997, page 254).

This particular knowledge alone should create in us the recognition that we cannot entirely exist of ourselves, and that there must be a single factor controlling our existence, one I believe, that is established with mathematical precision, taking into account the proportions of all that is around us, both in the heavens and on the Earth itself and which, includes a safe passage for the Earth's orbit through the universe.

This concept also appears to be the fundamental belief system of our ancestors, the ancient 'Sumerians', (circa 8000 - 2500 BC), who not only learned about their environment but also understood that the Earth was round. They even possessed knowledge of the Earth's dimensions, as well as the Earth's divisions of latitude and longitude, a knowledge, which I believe, was taught directly to them by the descended watchers, angels or aliens that existed at that time.

A more recent development within the scientific community is a return to the studying of ancient manuscripts, such as the Bible, and the Koran, including myths and legends in an attempt to re-evaluate the secrets of the past to determine our existence. Our entire future appears to depend more and more on our knowledge of the past. Indeed one man of old, named Isaiah, made a significant reference to this very same fact, which he framed in his writings when he wrote, in his 'challenge to the nations', that the wise men of this world "should produce their cause and bring forth strong reasons for their arguments against their knowledge of the past or their understanding of the future". Furthermore, Isaiah challenged them to demonstrate their knowledge asking them to declare just who it is that controls the events of this universe and what precisely are the former things. He even derides the nations by asking them not only to explain the past but also to consider what *precisely* may be the things that shall come hereafter, what is the future? He concludes his statement with the concept that, if the nations are able to see and do these things, for example, "reach into the past and tell the future backward", then they will be considered 'truly gods'. However, since we do not readily possess such knowledge of both the good and the evil in these matters, therefore we all shall be truly dismayed (Cited in: Isaiah chapter 41 v 21-29). Such profound works of wisdom are full of the richness of knowledge hidden in the text, which reveal a science that only now we are beginning to perceive with a measure of clarity in the form of precessional time travel.

How great and how many are the arguments for the existence of man? We are constantly being told that the universe was created in a big bang, which spread outwards from some central core. This theory may explain in part, the possibility of an expanding universe but nevertheless, it does nothing to satisfy or explain the existence of mankind or, of the Earth itself, in what appears to be a lonely existence among the many planets of the universe. In fact, it appears that modern science confirms to us that the universe is lacking life in the sense that, we can find no form like ourselves to communicate with. Is it entirely possible, that with a universe so vast as the one in which we live that we are the sole beneficiaries of a lonely existence?

That the human race is unique, I have no doubt, but that we are entirely alone is preposterous to say the least! Furthermore, the contentions for the ancient belief that mankind is the product of created beings such as Adam and Eve, though fantastic as this may seem to us today, does offer a conclusive remedy for our existence. 'We are not alone' also advocates a ready mechanism for the unexplainable events currently being observed with reports about UFO's, Alien Abduction and other equally strange phenomena.

Many scientists however, are becoming increasingly disillusioned by the established views constantly being put forward about our existence and as such, are of the opinion that our world is the product of a creator. If then, we are truly alone, how can we save ourselves from the fate that awaits us? Surely we are without hope and entirely undone if as many people say, "There is no God!" Here hangs the demise of nations and the fate of the world!

Interestingly enough, Astro-physicists point out that life in the main appears to have had little or no effect on the universe as a whole. These points appear to contrast with Enoch's view when he reveals that life changes within the universe as a whole, are a direct result of sin. He indicates that this is caused initially by stars that failed to keep their places (known as wanderers), and secondly, by the behaviour of mankind being influenced by the existence of beings known as the watchers, who descended to Earth in the days of Jared prior to the flood.

In *'The Anthropic Cosmological Principle'*, (by F. Tippler and J. D. Bower), it is suggested that if life were to die out at some stage, that the effect on the universe would, in their opinion, be negligible rather than end in a big bang (Cited in: Jeffrey 1997). However, this begs the question as to why and how the universe brought life into existence in the first place? Naturally, this tends to swing the pendulum of debate toward the religious hypothesis and the possibility of a creator God, which the scientific community refutes.

It appears to me that the scientific faculties omit the religious hypotheses from their theories about the universe, because they are somehow incapable of reaching a conclusive understanding of the construction of the universe and how it came into existence in the first place, simply because, the faculty cannot reason with the religious hypothesis, which mankind began with.

Instead, they prefer, as always, to expound their philosophical methodologies in the style of cyclic theories as exemplified by: which came first, 'the Chicken or the Egg', because these theories enable circuitous reasoning, by which means they become the sole providers of the conclusive hypothesis for the understanding our existence. Nevertheless, when considering the religious hypotheses in light of the chicken or egg universal arguments, the cosmos and the questions of life may not be too difficult to examine. In my opinion, the religious hypothesis embraces the possibility that the universe occurred sequentially as six major parallel events evolving into a single universal existence culminating in the chicken and egg arriving together, which is entirely feasible as suggested by the scriptures (Genesis Ch. 1 v 6-13).

This then would be a true act of creation involving a series of processes, as suggested by the scriptures, and which has become a universal principle of division and multiplication linked to a system of replenishment and refreshing a fact also suggested by the law of periodic change implied by M. Cottrell's study of *'Solar Radiation and Sunspot Cycles Theory'*. In particular his section on Catastrophe and Destruction in which he demonstrates the effects of solar radiation in conjunction with electromagnetic activity leading to changes in space and on the Earth (Cotterell 1995, pages 254 & 272). If this were plausible, then the problem of our existence would be to consider the pattern of these things, to determine, which was female and which was male. For example, that which is in the firmament above the heavens, is masculine.

If then, the laws of nature are the same as the laws of God, then science must accept something of the religious principle at work, as this provides a stable environment for establishing the existence of life in the universe and on Earth itself, in the first place. Through archaeological studies of the past, we are beginning to piece together the fragments of a long forgotten history in which it is becoming clearer that at certain periods, (approximately 22,700 BC - 11,000

BC), a number of catastrophic events have taken place that destroyed life.

More terrifying than this realisation, is the concept that such an event may occur again! The ancients recognised these cataclysmic events as a form of 'First Judgement' for all living things and have predicted in their writings and secret texts that at some time in the future there will be a 'Final Judgement' for mankind. Enoch predicts this judgement to happen after seventy generations have occurred, which in my reckoning is about 25,480 years, based on the numbers supplied by Enoch and is said to be the result of fire rather than water. Enoch was said to be a man, 'who walked with God' and he states: "And the Lord said unto me: "Observe... these heavenly tablets, and read what is written thereon, and mark every individual fact" (Cited in: Charles 1997, page 107).

If ever there was a time to watch and to observe, surely this period in which we are living must be such a time? The prophets and the seers of old wrote down in a coded form the secrets of the knowledge they possessed concerning the future of mankind and it was kept hidden for a time when men would once again be searching for the truth about their existence, which is out there in the universe! The truth that we are not alone. The truth that we are about to come to judgement again, unless we can truly 'see' and 'hear' and 'obey' that ancient word that comes to us all from across the universe. Unless we can read the heavenly tablets for ourselves and understand what is written on them, then our hope has faded.

Over the last ten years or so, men like Gilbert and Bauval, Graham Hancock, Robert Temple and Maurice Cotteral, have made similarly incredible suggestions concerning a number of ancient studies such as the pyramids at Giza and the historical remains of the Mayans. For example: Beauval's star correlation theory of the constellation of Orion, (which demonstrates a knowledge of precession designed to take us back to the days of Noah), *'The Orion Mystery'*, (1994) and most importantly M. Cotterell's studies of the Mayan calendar and his discovery that the world may end in circa 2012 AD. *'The Mayan Prophecies',* (1995). These skilful writers have attempted to re-fuel the debates and secrets of the past to a wider, yet very interested audience that at no time in the past would have ever been able to observe or learn the true secrets long kept hidden from the world by the establishment.

But what greater secret has been kept hidden from the world than this? Is it, that angelic beings called Watchers actually came to Earth in the days of Jared prior to the first judgement flood and the evidence of their existence lies at the very foundation of ancient history and in recent years, the re-appearance of UFO's since 1947, is somehow inextricably connected with the second judgement predicted by Enoch, that includes the return of these aliens in the last days. If, as I have already suggested, there is such a thing as a conspiracy against the human race and therefore a conspiratorial cover-up regarding the existence of UFO's and Aliens, then what exactly might be the reasons for this?

The involvement, primarily of the Roman Church and subsequently world governments, provides a range of possible reasons for the non-disclosure of the truth of alien existence from the public domain. A suggestion also put forward by numerous UFO researchers and other writers, and links this cover-up to religious, political, social and economic reasons.

Moreover, the question of religion and how the likely effects of alien existence, may heavily impact upon the masses, is considered detrimental, if religion cannot find plausible explanations to justify such existence, (something that the Enochian Legacy is attempting to do), because the context of religious beliefs as well as the lack of physical evidence makes it complicated and religious leaders of all denominations would find it extremely hard, (if not remotely impossible), to come to terms with such implications. After all, the idea of 'extraterrestrial intelligence' existing in the universe may provoke numerous problems for believers of all denominations and for Christianity as a whole.

It has also been suggested, that the Church may have a problem equating the possibility that God's work of redemption from original sin, might also apply to aliens or angels. It has been noted that the Vatican has already begun to put forward its own method of indoctrination in order to prepare its people for the acceptance of alien life. Members of the Catholic Church are expected to come to terms with the soon-to-be-made 'Official Announcement', by governmental agencies, about the existence of extraterrestrial intelligences and which, for two-thousand years or more, the Vatican has suppressed.

Recently the Vatican and its Jesuit partners have invested billions in the construction of the world's largest MGIO/VATT telescope using a tandem process optical system observatory, based at Mount Graham in Arizona, USA, in conjunction with The Max Planck Institution for Radio Astronomy, Sub-Millimetre Wave Telescope. Apparently, the participation of the Vatican Observatory in the MGIO is completely consonant with all public statements of Pope John Paul 111. This new telescope will enable scientists to see ten times further into the universe than ever before.

On the orders of the Pope they are instructed to seek out the 'Fingerprints of God' in order to establish the existence of planetary systems capable of sustaining life. Furthermore, the Pope's new indoctrination process called 'Speculative Theology' is designed to enable the church to respond to new discoveries in space and therefore, can be used to reinforce faith as opposed to undermining it. The real question here is why now? Why is the Catholic Church suddenly interested in extraterrestrial life and the search for ET? The church libraries are full of evidence long suppressed by past Papal authorities that have successfully done so for over two thousand years. It is certainly not a coincidence.

A parallel has been drawn in which NASA, the international space centre, has attempted to suppress information from the public domain and has also produced similar documentation including policies for the study of 'extra-solar life' of which the Papal document is only a fraction.

NASA may also be deeply involved in the suppression of the Enochian fragments regarding the truth of alien existence whilst at the same time spending billions searching the cosmos for their point of origin.

Could this be the real cause behind the establishment of the American 'Star Wars Program' known as 'Global Defence'? In my opinion, global defence serves no real purpose except for the possible suppression of nations, if, as they would have us believe, we are alone in this universe.

If however, the opposite is true and we are not alone in the universe after all, then it is plausible to consider that NASA has discovered the extra-terrestrial's point of origin, then global defence becomes more practical.

Did NASA get its information on their point of origin from the alien beings captured during the Roswell incident of 1947? Was the reason for placing the Hubble Telescope in space, also the means of establishing a clear view of the Alien's point of origin? If so, then the world would require the means to defend against attack from universal forces of unknown alien presence. Some may wish to interpret this differently. However, the Enochian Fragments are so profoundly put together with regard to details of the existence of alien intelligence, that it is impossible to ignore it.

Alien life and therefore alien intelligence has been discovered. The information concerning the evidence of this discovery has been locked away and suppressed until recently. At the same time, the impression has been purposely created to deflect attention in the form of religious and political upheaval on a worldwide scale, to enable consolidation of the evidence and purposely hide the truth from the public domain.

The impending 'New World Order' is consistent with the discovery of alien intelligence and has its roots back in the middle east and in particular, Palestine. It is consistent with prophetical, historical, geographical and political data and manuscripts dating back centuries. Among these is the *book of Revelations* and *the book of Daniel*, which confirm the ideology of the existence of 'a one-world order', including alien beings (Daniel ch7 & Revelations ch12 & ch13), after which, 'The Church' becomes triumphant. Should the world remain ignorant of these facts? The existence of alien beings and UFO's can no longer be denied regarding the evidence, which is just too overwhelming. In fact, it is highly feasible that the reason why suppression of the evidence is no longer possible, is that the aliens themselves have their own agenda for making known their own existence. Furthermore, why the Catholic Church should need to put forward its own indoctrination process for the 'gradual acceptance' of life elsewhere in the universe is a mystery. Incidentally, 'Gradualism' is not just a policy confined to the

Catholic church but is a policy which has for many years formed the basis of at least five other policies initiated by the 'Fabian Society', who are the backbone of British governmental politics and in particular, The Labour Party.

When we read the Bible for ourselves and study its writings closely, we discover that its pages are forever full of references and information about alien existence. For example, The Living God, as opposed to gods made of wood and stones which are the works of men's own hands, or discussion about angels and arch angels as well as that of 'fallen angels'. This subject is thoroughly debated in other sacred manuscripts such as the Vedic literature, confirming unquestioningly, the existence of such otherworldly beings. Why then is it so difficult for religious leaders to believe what is recorded? What is more, why should they go to great lengths to cover it up?

Recently, a former British Prime Minister was interviewed about these self-same issues and agreed that there should be a cover-up 'because aliens do exist' and stated that 'no matter what happens, you cannot tell the people', (Cited in: Bruni 2000).

No matter what the truth finally becomes, I believe that religious and spiritual phenomenon are both equally profound and important to our existence as well as the need for spiritual identity. Therefore, I believe it to be of the utmost importance, in the need to establish openly, that we are not alone in this universe after all.

Our refusal to accept the existence of otherworldly forces at work around us has seriously limited our capacity to deal openly with the possibilities proposed by recent UFO sightings and alien abductions.

Our religious upbringing as well as our development of scientific, rational, philosophical and psychological explanations for the existence of life around us, means that we shall continue to be duped by the unknown throughout our universe unless we can openly admit to the truth of their existence. If we cannot tell the truth, then alien abductions and animal mutilations will also continue to occur among us with no means available to stop it.

"... Go ye, Enoch,
say to the watchers of heaven: ...
wherefore have ye left your high,
holy, and eternal heaven,
and lain with women,
and defiled yourselves
with the daughters of men,
and taken to yourselves wives,

... though ye were Holy, Spiritual,
living the Eternal Life,
you have defiled yourselves
with the blood of women,
and have begotten (children)
with the blood of flesh".

(The Book of Enoch: xv.2; page 42).

CHAPTER TWO

The fall of the Angels & the Demise of Mankind

"And it came to pass when the children of men had multiplied upon the face of the Earth that in those days were born unto them beautiful and comely daughters. But certain of the Angels, the children of heaven, saw and lusted after them. And so it was that these Angels having left their heavenly abode, descended to Earth and (traded their secrets) or took of the daughters of men, all that they chose". (Charles 1997, page 34).

For centuries, the idea of 'other-worldly beings' visiting our planet or existing in some other dimension, on or near our planet, is one that has been frowned upon and scoffed at, by those who supposedly are wiser among us. Most official organisations, from priests to governmental ministers and from scientists to military leaders, including the media at large, prefer to classify UFO's and similar phenomenon to that of ghosts and sea monsters. They consider that the apparent sightings of such absurd phenomenon can be safely ignored or dismissed because the likelihood of their existence does not appear to conflict with the mainstream events of life in general.

However, the evidence for the existence of strange supernatural beings continues to occur throughout the world as Author, Walter Evans-Wentz for example, demonstrates in his book *'The Fairy Faith in the Celtic countries'* in which, he concludes that the factual and scientific evidence of supernatural beings is overwhelming (Cited in: Wilson 1998, page 103). In fact it is on record that other writers such as Paracelsus of the sixteenth century also concluded that the evidence for 'Otherworldly Beings' existing in some other dimension is real. Naturally, the Church has sought to quell this evidence over the years.

Indeed, no other institution has had such a major influence in controlling our beliefs more than the Church. This very powerful and persuasive authority has secretly kept the truth concerning the origins of mankind hidden from the world. Today this role, in conjunction with many other established religions, is taken up by Governments, military and secret organisations, in a continuing bid to conceal the truth about alien existence, from the public domain.

In 1994, Dr Brian O'Leary of Princeton University, openly discussed this point at the International Forum of New Science, when he stated that the Secrecy Apparatus of the US Government, for example, has kept from the public; "UFO and Alien Encounter information. This secrecy apparatus with regard to Aliens, UFO's, Mind Control Techniques, Genetic Engineering, Free-Energy Systems, Anti-Gravity Propulsion Systems and other such secrets.... have been kept hidden in some kind of 'Cosmic Watergate' for the past fifty years or more" (Cited in: Seller 1997, page 14). Why? You may well ask! The answer is not easily defined. However, despite government attempts to keep the lid on this strange cargo of events there is enough written evidence filtering down to the public domain as laws restricting access to this secret information are now being changed.

Furthermore, there is startling evidence being discovered in ancient manuscripts, such as the Vedic writings with references to flying cars and lightning bombs that fire bolts of lightning, and the Bible such as the book of Ezekiel for example, in which precise, but accurate information about the history of our existence as well as the evidence for the existence of alien races in space, and in our atmosphere, is being properly understood.

In fact, humanity has been deprived of deliberately suppressed information that has been locked away from ordinary people until now and it is only since the late 1990's that more people are beginning to show an interest in the subject. They are demanding to know the truth about UFO's and because of this, more manuscripts and governmental documents are being accessed. Opportunities to unlock the secrets of the past are now being given access to government secrets ranging from Crop Circles to Alien visitations.

The idea of 'Angels' for example, is one such secret that has been with us for a very long time; in fact, just about as long as the belief in 'Demons' too. Nevertheless, what evidence is there to support this concept? Author Nick Pope (1997), explores this same aspect of

Alien Abduction in his books *The Uninvited,* in which he draws a number of relevant parallels about the experiencers involvement within the abduction scenarios, including some discussion on mental health issues with particular regard to hypnotic regression. Some experts believe that 'sleep paralysis' may be the original cause. Author Colin Wilson in his book *Alien Dawn* also explores the reality of this phenomenon from various angles in which he considers the evidence for alien existence. According to Wilson, the scientist and magician Paracelsus, suggests that there is a whole class of supernatural beings residing in other dimensions between God and Man. He describes their apparent order as Gnomes, Nymphs, Dwarfs, Sylphs, Salamanders or Serpent Beings and Giants known as the Nephillim. In his references to supernatural beings, he suggests for example, that these beings may appear at will in any shape they choose. They may appear as small or tall, handsome or ugly, and furthermore Paracelsus argues that sometimes these beings can inflict severe penalties including death and there is genuine proof of this (Cited in: Wilson 1998, page 99).

In the Bible, throughout the early chapters of Genesis, it is indicated that other beings exist higher than we do. In Genesis chapter six, it is written that these 'beings' are the sons of God and that the human race is descended from them in heaven.

In 1917 AD, a man called R. H. Charles translated and wrote into English a little fragment of written text, which was discovered hidden away in the British Museum by the Reverend M. R. James. This fragment is known as the Book of Enoch. It describes the thoughts and ideas from ancient sources. This book contains some important information relating to our future and in particular it contains evidence of a race of beings descended from somewhere in heaven. Furthermore, this book actually gives their names (Cited in: Charles 1997, page 35).

The Book of Enoch describes the original purpose of their descent as well as the transactions of these alien beings, including the trading of skills, writing, sacred geometry and mathematics, building skills, medicines and magic rites (Cited in: Charles 1997, page 89). Clearly, this book has been kept from public view until much recently. It is interesting to note that Erich Von Daniken, author of a number of books on the subject of UFO's and ancient monuments, also asks the question:" Why do the worlds oldest libraries, appear to be secret libraries?" On the issue of gaining access to particular works for further study, he asks, "What are these people afraid of?" (Cited in: Daniken 1997, *According to the Evidence*). This is an observation I too have made over the years when requesting certain specific works of reference on this and many related subjects including specific works about the history of the Church and Church practices. Could the UFO sightings of 1947 to the present day have influenced the public release of this book and other ancient manuscripts normally kept hidden from public viewing?

In his writings, Enoch admonishes humanity to "observe everything that takes place in the heavens" (Cited in: Charles 1997, page 32). He especially points out how, that at the present times, (e.g. the times of his writing), that the system of the universe surrounding the Earth, does not change its orbits. Indeed, he further calculates that the order of the Sun, Moon, and Stars all rise and set in their orders and, within their set seasons. They do not, "Transgress against their appointed orders" (Charles 1997, page 32). In this matter, Enoch is quite emphatic about his revelation regarding the heavenly luminaries. In fact, he continues to state in the same section of text:

"Behold you the Earth, and give heed to the things which take place upon it from the first (*day*) to the last, how steadfast they are, (*the luminaries*), and how none of the things upon the Earth change. All the works of God appear unto you" (Cited in: Charles 1997, page 32). Our observances of these things include understanding the times and the seasons, both the summer and the winter.

Enoch adds: "See what 'His' works are and note all the tasks that these accomplish for him... As God hath ordained so it is done." (Cited in: Charles 1997, page 32).

In contrast to this fine balance of the order of the Earth and Heavens, Enoch turns his attention to the nature and order of Man, as well as the spiritual relationship involving certain fallen angel beings that, according to Enoch, is the primary cause behind the fall of mankind.

Furthermore, Enoch writes a little vehemently, that this unearthly relationship, including the gross misconduct of humans and in particular, the conduct of the Angels themselves, have affected the order of the universe as well as the heavenly luminaries and ultimately their seasons. Other prophets have told similar revelations that indicate to us all the seriousness of this endeavour and what great responsibility we have for ensuring that we do **not** transgress the natural boundaries of law and order created by God, for to do so, brings down the wrath of God upon us!

Enoch states that: "in these things we have not been steadfast and true... nor have we done the commandments of the Lord, but have turned away and spoken proud, haughty, and hard words" (Cited in: Charles 1997, page 33). Why does Enoch say this? It is because '**we**', think we know better than God. In fact, because of the fall of man from God's holy presence, mankind fails to acknowledge his own fallibility and has attempted therefore, to become 'his own god'. Such is the audacity of our fallen nature. This is the selfsame error that befell the watcher called Azazel.

The Bible paints a similar picture (Genesis 6 v 1-7). The only exception being, that any of the details relating to the involvement of the '*Angels*' in the process of our demise, and which, might cause the facts surrounding the fall of mankind to become a more accurate and compelling piece of information concerning our past, has been expertly masqueraded from the original sources of biblical text.

This action serves to create a greater mystery than may have been intended and prevents a clearer understanding of the truth surrounding the fall of man, and subsequently man's behaviour, which is the result of this unearthly union with alien beings from 'another world'.

Who is responsible for this masquerade against humanity? The Roman Church perhaps? History tells us that it was the Romans under the control of the senate that attempted to have all the 'Christians' killed in order to contain their newfound revelations, and to stem the rapid increase of believers after the death of Jesus Christ, but later in history, The Roman Church had risen to a place of power in the Roman world and had consistently and cleverly, contrived to absorb and control the Christian faith and suppress it from within.

The Roman Church has sought to infiltrate Christian principles, doctrine and lifestyles in an attempt to eradicate or change the written word of God into something of a mystery story. During the reign of Constantine, the Roman Church sought to collect information and religious relics relating to the past and in particular, to Christianity in its then present form. This was a bid to control and dominate the effectiveness of this new biblical religion upon the then known world.

The Roman Church, deceptively set about to recreate the past and all its historic secrets which mirrored Rome's Pagan beliefs and rituals, and by this means, they could control the religious influence of the new doctrine of believers, which had at that time, a major influence throughout the Roman world and beyond.

Enoch also predicted that, "In those days **you** (The Church & State), shall make your names an eternal execration unto all the righteous and because of you, shall all who curse, curse" (Cited in: Charles 1997, page 33). The papacy and the Church of Rome have inserted their own paganistic ritual beliefs into the scriptures. Through this action, they have ensured the continuity of 'their faith' and effectively tried to delay the purposes of God. They have consistently undermined world beliefs and in doing so have Romanised two thirds of the world.

Europe and its modern societies is the ultimate product of this invasion of Rome, and today we have become the product of this legacy of Rome. Adolf Hitler also recognised how effective Roman influence had become and he too, exploited this ideology for power and world domination in the form of his 'SS elite'. The very foundations of the New World Order, which includes the EEC and the USA, are based on the very same Roman political dogma that is currently written into the 'British and foreign pact'. This ideology of Roman rule is disguised in document form under the heading, 'The Treaty of Rome', which a number of nations have signed up to.

Furthermore, America's capital city, Washington DC, is known secretly as 'little or New Rome' (Ovason 2000, page 9). For many years, people have tried to guess at the identity of the man whose name is a number as indicated in the book of revelations, and have suggested a link with Rome, which is a city built on seven hills. Yet Ovason's discovery, concerning the secret Zodiac of Washington DC, reveals that this city is also built on seven hills and that this city, is also called 'Rome'. If so, could the man whose name is a number, also be based here? Furthermore, the existence of Roman ideology forming the basis of western society, having been built into the fabric of our cities, both here and in the USA, is intriguing, especially in the light of prophecy concerning books like Revelations. If this is not a clear indication for a prescription of Roman rule down the ages then we have misread the "signs of the times" (Matthew 16 v 3 & Matthew 24).

The world seems oblivious to recognise demons at work, although its libraries are full of books about their existence. It would seem that they only give credence to such beings in an abstract sense of the word demons, as and when it suits them. Enoch says: "Believe therefore, ye righteous, that the sinners **will** become a shame, and perish in the day of unrighteousness... and the Angels of heaven shall rejoice over your destruction" (Cited in: Charles 1997, page 138).

What then is the 'great truth' that has been kept from the world and from believers? How can we know for certain that it is 'the truth' and not another lie? The fact is, as already discussed earlier; there is sufficient evidence throughout the history of the world, to support the words of Enoch! Indeed, true believers will acknowledge this, that God never does anything without first revealing it to someone who will not only have appreciation for it, but also a true understanding of, 'The Word of God', as well as place upon it the correct values that such revelation imposes. This is one of the first revelations of His abiding presence in the affairs of men.

Enoch proceeds to tell us, on the basis of this same revelation of God, that in the generation of his father Jared, he had a vision in which, some of the Angels of Heaven transgressed the word of the Lord: "Behold they commit sin and transgress the law of Heaven, and have united themselves with the 'women of the Earth' and do commit sin with them and have even married some of them and have even had children by them" (Cited in: Charles 1997, page 34).

The result of this unification between angels and man is great bloodshed throughout mankind's history and development. The knowledge and skills of war, chivalry, heraldry, machines, writing, medicine and witchcraft, were exchanged for the ubiquitous favour of women. Here is the ancient record of *the X-Files*, and the truth is not only out there, because "as in the days of Noah, so shall it be in those days, when the Son of Man will come (Matthew 24 v 37)."

Firstly, this suggests that there will be a revival of a certain climate of change, which will mirror the same period of change experienced in the days of Noah as a result of events which occurred in Jared's day and which resulted in an antediluvian judgement. Can we afford to ignore this statement?

Secondly, I will remind the reader that according to Enoch, a second judgement will occur around 25,480 years after the first judgement, because of man's desire to increase in violent and destructive behaviour. In the reckonings of Enoch this final period of judgement began on August the tenth, 2001 and is known as the last days. Interestingly, the author Colin Wilson examines this same apparent concern, with regard to human violence and destructive behaviour, in his book *Alien Dawn*, and also suggests, that this same point of concern was put to 'abductees', by their alien captors. Should the governments of this world then, as a direct result of their policy making, continue to ignore or condone this aspect of human behaviour to our detriment? Society is being constantly undermined as the drive for change is accelerated. Sacred and healthy social values are being lost amidst a widening sea of uncertainty and an ever-increasing circle of fear. We are heading for a breakdown in law and order in our society and replacing this with a state of lawlessness as violence and crime becomes rife in our lands.

Is it any wonder, that The Seventy Generations, (25480 years) predicted by Enoch is almost at an end? What final encounters await us if we fail to heed the warning signs? Furthermore, just who are these alien visitors, where do they come from, and what is their true nature and purpose for being here? Are they responsible for the increase in violence experienced throughout the world or, are they here to stop it? If so, when?

"... And Uriel said to me:
'here shall stand the Angels
who have connected themselves
with women
and their spirits
assuming many different forms,
are defiling mankind,
and shall lead them astray' ..."

(The Book of Enoch: xix 1; page 45).

CHAPTER THREE

A brief encounter with the unknown

And it came to pass when the children of men had multiplied themselves upon the Earth, that in those days were born beautiful and comely daughters. However, the Angels, the children of heaven, saw and lusted after the women of men that they said to themselves: "Come let us choose us wives from among the daughters of men and by them let us beget children also" (Cited in: Charles 1997, page 34).

And Semjaza was their leader, who said: "I fear you will not indeed agree with me to do this deed and that I alone shall have to pay the penalty for this great sin." Moreover, they were in all about two hundred who descended on the summit of Mount Hermon in the days of Jared (Cited in: Charles 1997, page 34).

When I was a young lad of about fourteen years of age, myself and several of the children from the estate where I lived, would often play in the woods nearby. In those days, steam trains would run along the railway tracks that divided our estate from the woodlands, which stretched out beyond the rear of our homes.

This was also a time when I remember how we used to run down a small narrow pathway that ran parallel to the tracks upon which steam trains would pass. The trains would halt at a point where the path ended abruptly. Often the steam trains would sit, waiting for the signalman from the nearby signal box, less than a quarter of a mile away, to change the signal from red to green, allowing the train to pass on its journey to the West Country.

As youngsters, we would often sit on the wire fencing that was erected to keep people off the tracks and any subsequent railway property, which of course, it never did. Here we would talk to the drivers of the trains or the passengers that would be leaning out of the attached carriages. It was great fun for us. By now, things were beginning to change. It seemed all of a sudden really.

One day there were steam trains chugging through the countryside where we lived and the next they were gone. Eventually, as the years passed by, the memory and the physical proof of their existence faded with the ripping up of the tracks. Today, there is no evidence of these trains ever having been there. A short distance from the place where the railway lines once stood is a modern method of transportation. A highway for traffic built somewhere between 1967 and 1974.

I remember, when as I said, I was about fourteen years of age. The day was crisp and fresh at the latter part of the summer holidays. I had agreed to meet some friends over in the woods that Saturday morning, it had been chilly with rain from the night before and the ground was damp. The sun had not been fully exposed yet.

I walked down the narrow pathway that divided the houses from the railtracks and climbed over the thin wire fencing. Once across the tracks, there followed a further climb over a second fence barrier on the other side of the tracks, where I entered a small stretch of open ground that lay between the railway line and the woods beyond. I then walked along the pathway that ran across the narrow strip of 'L-shaped' field that led to the entrance of the first wood or 'lightwood', as we liked to call it.

Here, I stood, listening in the silence of the morning for the familiar sounds of my friends playing in the woods, but I heard nothing except the chilled damp autumn-like breeze and the birds singing in the treetops.

After a few minutes, I entered the woods, passing by the old familiar oak tree that stood alone and proud, marking the entrance to my right, and bounded by a low barbed-wire fence that stretched out along the edge of the woods close to the pathway.

Further along, the pathway divided into a fork to the right and to the left of yet another much younger oak tree. Again, I halted to determine the sounds before me in an attempt to decide which path to take. The trees were well spaced out enabling me to survey this area for some considerable distance, as I stood alone, listening for my friends. Again, nothing but the silence of the woods and there were no birds singing this time, which I thought a little strange as I pressed onward.

I took the path to my right that followed the barbed-wire fencing. Shortly after, the path descended on a soft gradient wending its way down to a lower plateau some distance from the second, but slightly darker woods beyond. Eventually, I began to hear the voices of those familiar sounds, which I had eagerly listened for earlier, and soon discovered my friends playing war games in the soft grey earthy floor that was mingled with white and blue sand.

Here and there throughout the lightwood, were masses of ferns that we would pull up and use for making dens, or for camouflage, which is the sort of things that youngsters like to do. After a while, another group of kids joined us, some of whom were slightly younger than we were. It was about 10.00 am. The sun was beginning to brighten now and it felt much warmer. We continued to play war games using acorns for grenades and aptly shaped sticks for rifles.

One of the lads divided us into two teams, the hunters and the hunted, and so we played. After several hours of running about, hiding and crawling around among the ferns, or climbing trees and capturing our enemy, we fell about in an open space on the plateau where there were fewer trees and began to get our breath back from the morning's exercise. Neither side truly winning of course.

At this point, the younger ones decided they had had enough and were going home for lunch, as it was roughly 1 o'clock by now. Within a few minutes, the group of youngsters had disappeared back up the hill towards the great oak that stood at the entrance to the woods. Those of us that remained watched them as they slowly walked out of sight and wondering whether or not we should do the same.

Whilst we continued to debate our next move, the group that had left us about ten or fifteen minutes before, returned in a hurry like they had just had a major fright of their lives. Some of them were in tears, and deeply distraught. We ran toward them, moved by what might be ailing them. Questioningly, we managed to coax them into revealing the nature of their apparent fear. They all began shouting or screaming at once. We tried to calm them down and start from the beginning, one at a time.

One of the lads, slightly taller than his peer group, began to explain what had happened to them. He said: "we had just 'gotten close to the great oak tree past the forked pathway and were about to exit the woods to cross the field when on our left, behind the oak tree, in the field, we saw a large orange globe. We stopped in surprise wondering what it could be. Then we became afraid, as it began pulsating around and we did not know what it was doing there. All we wanted to do was go home. We tried to go past it and as we did so, we ran out of the woods towards the railway line, but then it quickly followed us! This orange ball went right around in front of us and stood there so we could not get past it! When we turned and ran back into the woods the ball followed and went back round to where we first saw it! After a while we tried again, but the same thing happened, except this time it went right around to the giant pine tree that stands alone in the middle of the field. We just stood still on the path and then suddenly, it came straight towards us so we ran back into the woods to find you lot."

The friends that I had stayed behind with in the woods, thought that these lads who were telling us of their experience were actually making it up, after all, giant balls don't float around on their own. "It must be some kind of a trick...Somehow?" exclaimed one of them. I observed the small group of boys as they stood in front of us. As I did so, I noticed the evidence of fear in their faces as well as the tears on some and I concluded that they must have experienced something for them to be so scared like this.

"Why don't we go with them and see it for ourselves" I replied, to which they all agreed. So together, we ran back up the hill and past the forked pathway towards the great oak near the wood's entrance. Nothing was to be seen or heard of the orange globe the lads said they saw.

The tallest of them showed us the spot where the globe had apparently sat but we could see nothing to prove that anything had been there. Some of us climbed over the barbed-wire fencing to inspect the ground and surrounding bushes but again nothing damaged or disturbed to indicate the existence of the globe.

We asked the boys to show us the projection of the globe and how far they travelled out of the woods before it followed them and also to show us where it finally stood before chasing them back. This they did cautiously, as they were still very much afraid despite our reassurances.

As we walked out into the open, we espied an elderly lady walking her dog across the pathway toward the giant pine tree that stood alone in the middle of the field. This tree was a sort of halfway marker between the railway and the woods. It stood approximately ten to fifteen yards from the pathway and was on the right-hand side, as you exited the lightwood. I called out to the lady as she crossed in front of us and enquired as to whether she had observed anything strange in the field to which she replied "No". I thought to myself then, that I did not recognise her or her dog. Who was she and where did she come from? Stranger still, what was she doing walking her dog there? The reason for my thinking this was, that she would have had to get over the railway fencing to enter this area as we had always done so. The only gate to this field was down the slope behind the giant pine tree, which was the direction she was heading in and furthermore, where could she have walked the dog?

The area we searched was an L-shaped field that turned up towards the great oak and followed the course of the woods as far as the entrance to the second woods where it stopped. No one as far as I knew, ever walked in that section before, as the grass was boggy and full of brambles.

We all decided that whatever the boys imagined they saw was not evident now. Unanimously the events of that morning were tiresome and so we all agreed to meander home, crossing the railway line and walking down the narrow pathway past the gardens on our right and into the estate.

Before finally parting with the group, I spoke to the young boy who was still very much afraid and crying. I asked him to recap the story in his own words and to describe what he had actually seen. This he did and it was clear from his expressions that something real had affected him. He swore never to go into those woods ever again. He never did!

After many years had passed by, I would recall this moment. The picture of fear on the boy's face was a sight I will never forget, and every time I think about the unexplained UFO events and sightings that we so often read about, I am reminded of him and the impact this made on me.

Is it possible that invisible, magical forces can actually exist? Is it possible also that these influences can have such profound effect on humans and our surroundings? Is it possible also that these forces are the product of alien races or Angelic forces of light or dark? Why are we not educated about these strange yet re-occurring phenomena? Will we ever find the answers to these and other questions about alien existence? One thing I am certain of is that these paranormal/UFO incidents appear at times of great change and true to form, some time later, the landscape was changed. The railway was abandoned and the steam trains never came by any more.

The spot where the youngsters had witnessed the Orange Globe had now been transformed into a dual carriageway and access to the woods was now impossible. Was the UFO then a harbinger of change?

Did the district council's need to alter the environment somehow trigger this UFO response or visa versa did the UFO's need to change the landscape and environment trigger this same response in the local council? If so, how and why? What was so important about this particular environment that required this almost, geometrical change, in the landscape in the first place?

CHAPTER FOUR

"Mount Hermon by Mutual Imprecation"

Mount Hermon is a prominent but rugged mountainous area in the northeastern border of Palestine. It is situated very close to the border of Lebanon. The actual location of mount Hermon is at the southern tip of mountains known as the Antilibanus Mountains and it is the source of the river Jordan. Mount Hermon towers high above the ancient city of Dan.

The historical facts about Mount Hermon that I have been able to uncover, is that the Ammonites who dominated that region originally, actually refer to Mount Hermon as 'Senir' or 'Shinar.' Another interesting piece of information is that the Sidonians who lived on the West Side of the mountains, close to the sea, actually called Mount Hermon 'Sirius' or 'Sirion'. However, the biblical book of Deuteronomy indicates precisely that it was called 'Sion' (Duet. 4v48). This title must not be confused with the Mount Zion that is Moriah, upon which the City of David now stands, known as Jerusalem.

A Yarad is an ancient Hebrew/Aramaic word meaning 'Place of Descent' and can be used in connection with references to Mount Hermon. It is the place of going down, the place of first descent or to use an Egyptian phrase: "Tep Zepi" (The place of the first time) or the place of the first encounter with the angels of God. An account of this first descent concerning original alien contact is revealed in the book of Enoch, he also includes details of the beings involved, the numbers of those who descended, and their apparent purpose for choosing Mount Hermon as a landing site. Enoch tells us that this event occurred in the days of Jared when the Angels of Heaven first met with the people of Earth. The book of Enoch fully demonstrates this fact, that Earthlings were visited by beings from another world and that this meeting took place upon, and close to, the Antilibanus Mountains and in particular the region of Mount Hermon or "Mount Sion" as it is secretly known.

Could this differentiation between these two terms 'Sion' and 'Zion' be 'the truth' that the Church and other organisations have sought to suppress for so long; and is this also the truth that the disciples and the early Christians learned from Jesus? The truth, that there are beings from outer space who visited the Earth in the days of Jared and established a secret base called Sion. If so, then special consideration must be given when examining these points, because Mount Hermon was also the place that Jesus took his disciples to when Peter obtained his revelation of who Jesus really was. This place was called 'Caesarea Philippi', and is the source of the 'Jordan River', situated at the foot of Mount Hermon. Moreover, Peter gained his revelation of who Jesus was, after being questioned by Jesus as to whom other men said he was. Peter's reply was, that Jesus was none other than: "the Christ, the Son of the Living God" (Matthew Ch16 v 13), and it was to this specific revelation of Peter's, that Jesus stated that this revelation that He truly is the Christ, the Son of The Living God, was "The Rock", or 'The foundation' statement upon which, He would "build his Church" and that, "the gates of hell would not prevail against it" (Mathew Ch 16 v 16-18). Furthermore, This statement has for centuries, been the fulmination of gross misunderstanding and delusion within the church, because of the churches' failure to recognise the true 'Light of God' in this statement, even when they are staring directly at him, face to face. This is the stone of stumbling, which the wise men of the churches fall on because they have reckoned on Peter as the rock simply because his name means 'rock'. Even more astounding, is the fact that, this revelation concerning Jesus, as the true Son of the Living God, is also a slap in the face for the angels of darkness who brought the wrath of God to mankind when they first descended on Mount Hermon in the days of Jared some 22,700 years ago. If this were so, might this knowledge now offer some **genuine** hope of salvation and a clearer explanation for the existence of a living God, who says: "I am God and I change not" (Isaiah Ch 43 v 12, 45 v 22, 46 v 9, and Hosea Ch 11 v 9), and as the Son of God, that he is: "the same, yesterday, today and forever" (Hebrews Ch 13 v8).

When viewed in this context, the facts of this argument increase in strength and give greater definition and meaning to some of the things that Jesus both said and did.

However, when we link the statements of Jesus to those of Enoch we gain an even deeper insight into the background of all these events, and thus we have a broader picture of the realities involved in the whole alien/angel phenomenon.

According to the book of Enoch, Semjaza was the leader of the aliens who came down on Mount Hermon, described above. He was the one recorded by Enoch, who spoke to the ten captains under him and informed them of his intentions to visit Earth and to settle here, even marrying the human women and having offspring through them.

In his statement to the captains he says: "I fear you will not indeed agree to do this deed, and I alone shall have to pay the penalty of a great sin" (Charles 1997, page 34).

Here, Semjaza clearly indicates that his exposure to the daughters of men and his intentions of a lustful nature towards human women, is a sin: "which shall carry with it a great penalty of judgement upon it" (cited in: Charles 1997 page 35).

That judgement was the great flood recorded by Noah in Genesis chapter six verses one to seven, where Noah writes what God revealed to him. Note the opening statement. "And it came to pass!" This implies that God revealed his intentions before the events spoken by Noah: "And it came to pass, when men had multiplied upon the face of the Earth, and Daughters were born unto them, that the sons of God saw the daughters of men that they were fair and comely; and they (*Semjaza and his company*), took them wives of all which they chose (Charles 1997, page 34).

Dr Sitchin, an expert in Semitic, Hebrew and European languages as well as Old Testament and near-eastern archaeology, confirms that certain biblical accounts with regard to references about 'The Sons of God and The Nephillim', suggests, that these stories correspond with the beginnings of human history and can be found in ancient Sumerian and Egyptian records as well. He claims that in the Egyptian tradition, recorded by Herodotus, that a group known as the 'Neterus' were the fathers of the 'demi-gods' who were the giants, the resultant offspring through intercourse with human women (Cited in Charles Seller 2000, page 42).

Noah also reveals in his works, this same secret knowledge concerning the existence of the Nephillim as the offspring of alien collaboration. This knowledge was handed down to him from Enoch his Great Grandfather, who informed him of the reason for the impending judgement upon mankind, which would result from this unholy alliance by Semjaza and Azazael.

This demise created by the watchers, has caused serious consequences for mankind. The full effects of this action occurred in the days of Jared, somewhere between circa 22,700 - 17,100 B.C., prior to the birth of Noah and had not been fully recognised until the flood came and washed them all away. Noah and his family were the exception. The Bible indicates that a similar fate awaits modern man. Jesus said: "As in the days of Noah so shall it be when the Son of Man cometh" (Matthew Ch 24 v 37). However, the captains who were with Semjaza when he expounded his plot to them, all answered him and said: "Let us all swear an oath, and all bind ourselves by mutual imprecations not to abandon this plan but to do this thing." (Cited in: Charles 1997, page 34).

So it was that they all swore and there were gathered together at this time, two hundred of these watchers from space and thus, they descended on the summit of Mount Hermon of which they named it in the days of Jared, and made contact with the people of Earth at the foot of the mountain where the source of the Jordan River began its journey south.

"These are their names which followed: Semjaza who was the chief among them and the leaders or captains are Arakiba, Rameel, Kokabel, Tamiel, Ramiel, Danel, Ezeqeel, Baraqijal, Asael, Armaros, Batarel, Anael, Zaqiel, Samsapeel, Satarel, Turel, Jomjael, and Sariel. These were the officers over tens. All the others, together with them, took unto themselves wives and each chose for him one wife, and began to lay with them and to defile themselves with them" (Cited in: Charles 1997, page 35).

The trade off for this Earthly venture was the giving away of charms and enchantments, maps of the stars and maps of the Earth, as well as the knowledge of herbal medicine and other apparent secrets. Eventually their wives, whom they had taken, became pregnant and their offspring became giants.

Now when the giants grew of age, they became demanding and consumed all the acquisitions of men and when they could no longer be satisfied or sustained, the giants ran riot and turned against humankind and sought to destroy them. The giants began to kill off the animal populations: the birds, beasts and reptiles as well as the fish of the sea and rivers. Eventually the giants could no longer sustain themselves because of their recklessness. They began to fight, kill and eat each other.

Enoch explains that the spirits of these giants shall be called, "Evil Spirits upon the Earth" and that these spirits shall go about the Earth causing the following conditions affecting mankind: Afflictions, Oppressions, Destruction, Attacks on life, cause of battle and Warfare, as well as all works of destruction and chaos on the Earth, (cited in: Charles 1997, page 43).

Enoch describes the behaviour of these spirits in that they shall not eat nevertheless their hunger and thirst shall be such that they shall be the primary cause of all kinds of life-threatening offences against the human race, as described above.

The artist, William Blake, depicted many gory scenes demonstrating the full horror of the giants, in his paintings, is it possible then, that Blake was privy to the mysteries surrounding the secrets written by Enoch concerning the existence of the giants and what became of them?   If so, what other mysteries are still kept hidden from the public domain?

Furthermore, just what is the truth surrounding the mystery of the alleged UFO crash at Roswell, New Mexico in 1945? What is the truth concerning the spate of animal mutilations that have occurred in group incidences around the world, affecting horses, sheep and cows? What are the strange lights, often seen by witnesses, in the vicinity of these incidents? How do we explain the visual sightings of UFO's, by some witnesses, at the scene of some of these bizarre incidents? Where are the animal body parts that are taken and, for what purpose are these parts being taken? How does one explain the sighting of an orange globe-like object seen in woodland, which terrorised its witnesses? Furthermore, how can one explain the appearance of a mystery jump jet that almost landed on an estate and arrived out of thin air, or the daylight sighting of a UFO in almost the same spot a few years later? These are just some of the incidents explored in the following chapters.

CHAPTER FIVE

The mystery of the Harrier Jump-Jet

The summer holidays were always the highlight of my youth. I longed for nothing better than to while away the hours playing with my friends and enjoying the hot sunshine. Often, we would roam the countryside on foot or on our bicycles soaking up the fresh country air and having a jolly good time.

I remember that one year during the summer, our estate had been invaded by workers, lorries and machinery. They had cut a trench around the estate to lay pipes in; and either side of the trench had been piled up with soil and sand. As you can imagine, children love sand to play in and we were no different.

I remember, that whilst my friends and I were playfully messing about in the trench, I caught sight of a Jet struggling to stay in the air a short distance away. The most peculiar thing I noted about this was how it just appeared there out of nowhere! I do not know anything about jets really except to say that it should not have been there.

The estate where I lived had approximately sixty houses on it at that time and from the air the layout of the area appeared like the horns of a bull, or a very badly scrawled 'W' on the landscape. The houses were aligned in pairs in a kind of straight terrace opposite an 'L-shaped' field from which we could also view the village stretched out at a level below the estate.

Across this field, and in a dip at an angle from our house, was an old oak tree whose branches obscured part of the view towards the west of us. Beyond this, we could clearly see the cricket pitch further along in the village.

We played in the sand some twenty to thirty feet from my home. I had just climbed up onto the heaped-up sand excavated from the trench days earlier and as I did so, that is when I glanced up to see the Jet mysteriously appear above the fence line of the field, about sixty-to-seventy feet away from where I was standing.

The jet seemed to be a military style Harrier Jump Jet and I could also see the pilot clearly wrestling with the controls of the aircraft, trying to keep the jet off the ground. In his effort to do so, the nose of the plane was down slightly at first, and then went upwards slightly, in the struggle.

I watched intensely as the pilot nudged the plane forward, a little closer toward us, and it seemed as though he was about to come down on the ground. Had he done so at this point of my observation, his left wing would have crushed the wire fencing possibly throwing the jet onto its side.

I shouted to the lads who were with me. "Look at that, there is a jet about to land in the field." I pointed towards it as I did so, but my friends appeared oblivious to what I was seeing, which I thought peculiar at the time.

In almost the same instance the pilot began to get the nose of the plane up a little at an acute angle and as he did so, he turned the jet around to face the opposite direction towards the woods at the corner of the estate facing west-north-west approximately.

Having managed to stay in the air, the pilot tugged on the controls and the plane began to climb a few feet above the ground. Then at about twenty feet above the ground where it hovered, came an almighty loud bang that shook the earth on which we stood, and then it proceeded to climb even higher. The jet moved gradually forward and upward over the top of the trees and disappeared out of sight.

I have never forgotten that experience, but what was more important at that time, was the fact that my friends did not appear to get excited about this intrusion to their lives and no-one else, as far as I could tell, came out of their homes to investigate the stricken Jet, or the loud bang that followed.

I kept quiet about this incident and some time after I thought I may have imagined it but then what reason would I have had for this, since I was playing happily with my chums before this incident occurred? I had no previous thoughts to warrant an incident of this nature occurring and since I had no knowledge of this possibility, how could I? A mystery indeed, if that is what it is.

Years later, I discovered a book called the, *'Philadelphia Experiment',* about a similar instance involving the world's greatest scientist, Einstein, in a 1943 project on invisibility, and in which, it is also alleged, his apparent connection with a disappearing battleship, said to be an effect of Einstein's *'Unified Field Theory'*, in which, some form of degaussing experiment had apparently taken place in the Bermuda triangle, an area also said to be a UFO window, (Berlitz, 1979).

The Harrier Jump Jet, which I observed in the field on our estate all those years before, definitely had all the implications of a similar mystery attached to it. However, as a youngster I could do nothing more than take mental note of my observation in the hope that one day I might understand something about what I witnessed that day.

The experiences of such strange events in my life have led me on a lonely and complicated quest for truth. The past thirty years or so have been difficult, but I have sought to find the answers wherever I can find them. I have learned that there are many things in heaven and on Earth that need an explanation, but that what we are led to believe or know about, by those who seemingly are better equipped among us, are nothing short of lies.

**Concerning the watchers:
"These are the angels
who descended to the Earth
and revealed what was hidden
to the children of men,
and seduced the children of men
into committing Sin".**

(The Book of Enoch: xiv.2; page 85).

CHAPTER SIX

The things Mankind has learned to do

In the days of Jared, some two hundred and thirty-five years before the great flood, mankind was gradually introduced to beings from another world. Trading for the favour of women resulted in mankind learning about technology and medicine as well as astronomy and religion. For example, Azazel taught men how to make weapons such as swords, knives, and spears of metal, including shields for protection as well as breastplates. He even introduced men to the knowledge of metallurgy and the art of working with metals dug from the earth. He also taught the human race about the uses of antimony, and the beautifying of the eyelids (displayed by the ancient Egyptians). In addition, Azazel was the one who taught men about making bracelets and other metal ornaments made with costly stones and cleverly designed tinctures.

This knowledge led to the corruption of mankind and eventually crimes became rife. There arose much corruption and greed, fornication and godlessness, as humanity became corrupt in all its ways (Genesis Chapter 6).

Meanwhile, Semjaza taught mankind enchantments and herbal medicines and witchcraft, whilst Armaros taught a form of white witchcraft and how to undo spells and enchantments. Baraqiel taught the knowledge of the stars and astrology (the method or science of reading them).

Ezeqeel taught understanding and knowledge of the clouds and weather systems. Araqiel taught the signs of Earth's magnetic fields; and Shamsiel taught the movements of the sun, whilst Sariel taught the knowledge of the phases of the moon.

It was this knowledge that began a fine resumé for learning and expansion, which mankind had discovered at the hands of the alien and put into practice via their watchers' intervention. How these angels must have seemed like gods to the people of Earth in those days! According to Enoch, these Angels revealed (or taught), what was once secret or hidden, to the children of the Earth.

Here is the explanation which scientists and archaeologists of our time are seeking to understand. The question of how mankind, living in village-like settlements, could suddenly leap forward to building pyramids, and fortified cities and other large-scale projects.

The answer to this question comes from another world, and as Enoch reveals, men were visited by beings from outer space and *they* taught mankind all it knows today. All the Technology and Science of our world comes from that initial encounter with alien beings that descended in the days of Jared, and landed on the summit of Mount Sion, which we now know as Mount Hermon to this day.

This may seem impossible today, but this is the truth; and many in authority over us know this to be the truth. The evidence we are confronted with requires an answer. The ancient pyramid texts of Egypt contain similar references. The statues of Easter Island to the pyramids of Yucatan, and the pyramids of Egypt, along with many other sacred places around the globe, suggests that something other than human hands was involved in their construction. The evidence is undeniably there. Mankind was visited and has been consistently visited, by Aliens.

Temple, Bauval, Gilbert, Cotteral, Hancock *et al,* are right in their assumptions about the ancients of Egypt and Mexico and the authorities know it.

In particular, Temple, who places his scientific evidence for alien contact back as far as 5000 years ago, argues in his first book, *The Sirius Mystery* (1998), that a group of people called the 'Dogon' held secret connections with alien visitors from the constellation of Sirius. Temple reveals that the Dogon had information, suppressed into strange religious rituals surrounding Sirius, Sirius B and Sirius C (not yet discovered by modern astronomers), that identifies an alien connection with Sirius and he traces its history back 7000 years and even to 10,000 years to the Akkadians and Sumerians of the ancient Middle East (Temple 1998, page 54). His work on this subject is the greatest revelation to date, yet to be surpassed. His conclusions, though arrived at scientifically, are the same as mine, in that he also believes that aliens have visited the Earth in our distant past.

I cannot help but wonder what discoveries he could advance for us if he were to study the book of Enoch in the same way that I have done.

The Orion Mystery by Robert Bauval (1994), and *Heaven's Mirror* by Graham Hancock (1998), also reveal that these authors believe that ancient peoples left us a legacy of truth written upon the ground. These revelations can only be observed from the air or from space (as proposed by Daniken, Temple, myself and others), and that they demonstrate that the Earth truly is the footstool of God. For like any footstool ever made, are the patterns and clues of the heavens themselves, and which, can have only been constructed with knowledge of the stars. Who better to have done this than those who travelled among them thousands of years ago, before the days of Jared?

So, will the world continue to shut its own eyes to the truth that is out there and to the masses of physical evidence in our own backyard on mother Earth? On the other hand, will the world wake up from its slumber and finally acknowledge that we are not alone and that whoever it is that is out there in our universe must be embraced with an open mind? This we may need to do in order to establish worldwide recognition of a civilisation higher than ourselves, capable of travelling vast distances at the speed of light. Who are these travellers of the stars?

Enoch refers to these Angels as "The Watchers" and the Bible calls them the *"Elohim"* and it would appear that these same alien visitors were responsible for designing the megalithic sacred patterns and structures on the surface of the Earth and that human contact with these angels resulted in a form of worldwide seduction culminating in mankind being held responsible for their crimes against God and His laws, for which the human race was left with severe penalties and judgements.

Modern scientists however, have decided that if extraterrestrial life exists in our universe or elsewhere, that alien beings or Angels, would identify with a few simple rules for making contact with us, again this methodology is decided by us. How tunnel-visioned the mind of modern man has become, to think that those alien life forms would communicate with us in this way! These same scientists are incapable of accepting that contact has already been made with us through sacred megalithic patterns and that the evidence for this already exists not only in antiquity, but more recently since 1947; from a visitation of the first kind, to alien abduction, and from visual sightings on masse, to crop circles. What more evidence do we need than this?

Furthermore, there are many strange UFO stories such as that of 'Roswell', 1947 and 'Rendlesham Forest', December 1980, that we have been increasingly informed about since these dates, and that these stories serve to compound the concept that we are in touch with a higher, intelligent race of beings, who are truly out of this world.

The fact is, we cannot get to the heart of these matters with any real proof of their existence, because we are surrounded by those in authority that would "turn even the Truth of God into a lie", (Romans Ch 1 v 18 & 25) and much less so, that of alien life, visiting our planet. What do these authorities think about the climatic changes taking place in recent years and are they aware that these changes are a mirroring of the days of Noah as foretold by Jesus in the Gospels (Matthew 24 v 37)? Are these authorities also aware, that their deliberate attempts to induce major world changes through politically correct policies and current world thinking, is also responsible for the globalisation of lawlessness and the breakdown of traditional values that society once held sacred? The desire for a one world order and all that this entails, will lead to the scriptural fulfilment of the book of Revelations (Chapters: 17 v 11, 18 v 10, 21 v 8), in which, the kings of this world will have committed fornication not only through the seal of Rome (Ovason 1998, page 9), but also through the foundations of the new Babylon that is yet to become the ancient Phoenix of our modern world, rising from the ashes of that ancient Babylon, the Macedonia of Iraq. Is mankind being duped into believing that the sort of society the governments of this world are trying to bring about under a one-world order, is actually the result of the influence of these alien beings and fallen angels in which, the establishment of a world demise, brings about an act of ultimate judgement of the world? Perhaps this deliberation by those in league with such dark forces has more to do ultimately with the entrapment of the human soul and an impending hell than humans currently realise. If so, then belief in a living God might just be good cause for wanting to escape this world demise by calling upon his salvation.

"... And in those days
the Angels shall return ..."

(The Book of Enoch: lvi.5).

CHAPTER SEVEN

A Doorway to Other Dimensions

Scientists have developed a peculiar interest in the weather. In particular, they are studying the storm-based weather systems that develop rapidly. One aspect of particular interest to scientists is how lightning is formed and conducted. Recent studies have shown that lightning does not always behave as predicted by our past understanding of this subject.

In fact, lightning is now known to have at least two distinct possibilities. Scientists have observed that a common percentage of lightning strikes tend to be *"air to ground"* strikes, but closer studies have revealed that sometimes lightning is given off from the Earth in the form of *"ground to air"* lightning strikes.

This particular event was previously unknown with regard to lightning, which occurs when highly charged particles of hot and cold air meet and densely-formed clouds quickly appear surrounding these particles, trapping them into a pressurised weather system.

This system, when sufficiently charged, gives off a violent stormy reaction in which lightning occurs intensely. The noise of thunder occurs when the particles of highly charged air are fused together and lightning is formed. It is one of nature's most frightening yet dazzlingly spectacular light shows.

In the USA, a particular stretch of land known colloquially as *'Storm Alley'* appears to undergo an annual event of storms, hurricanes and tornadoes. In fact, this area of the American Continent is often referred to as *'Tornado Valley'* and a group of scientists (and others) set out to study the peculiar nature of these storm systems. They are called 'storm chasers', because these men and women risk their lives seeking out and getting right under the formation of the weather system. The scientists collect data by the use of technological instruments designed for this purpose. They then use this information to report to the weather centres. This information can be used to warn villages, towns and cities that may be in the path of these violent storm systems, should it be necessary to do so. The people may be evacuated, or they may take shelter in storm cellars built for this purpose.

Here in Britain, we have experienced the force of some of these weather systems, including mini tornadoes that run for a short distance overland, before disappearing as quickly as they are formed. Often, these storms are found at sea. They can develop over wide grass plains such as the Serengeti in Africa, or vast desert regions such as those found in the 'outback', in Australia. However, it is in America's Storm Alley that they occur with the utmost frequency and intensity. Here Tornadoes have been described as being over a mile wide with speeds of up to 200 miles per hour or more. These are among the most destructive of systems seen anywhere in the world.

On one occasion, I was standing on our back-door step with my family, including my mother, who was talking over the fence to our next-door neighbours, when I noticed, that a sort of low mist-like cloud was forming at the lower end of our back garden.

At this end of the garden, four more gardens ran across the bottom of it, so that if you imagined a 'T' shape, our garden would be the stem or shank of the 'T' with the other four gardens being the top of the 'T' shape. A short distance beyond these was a bit of waste-land, part of which had been made into a large car park. To the right of this was a single gorse bush, quite tall in size, and further to the right, still more gorse bushes and waste-land that came to a halt at the gardens further to the right of ours.

The houses at this point, ended at the foot of the railway line that ran across the top of the gorsy waste-land and the car park. This is the railway line that I spoke of in an earlier chapter that ran along by the woods and every part of my description could be viewed from our back door.

To the right yet again, one could view clearly the hills in the background. The mist-like cloud that formed, quickly became grey in colour, and appeared approximately some thirty feet or so off the ground. The mist continued to form until it came level with the large gorse bush described above.

In an instant, there was a huge bolt of lightning, very jagged like the teeth of a woodsman saw, which were several feet wide, and they were very large indeed.

The lightning appeared to go deep into the ground, right on the spot where the gorse bush was sitting. The brightness of the strike was very intense and appeared to stand still when it struck into the ground, lasting up to several seconds before disappearing. This was not all I observed, the gorse bush caught fire and was consumed.

The cloud remained for some time after the strike and no other lightning strikes occurred on that day. At the same moment the lightning struck the ground, I noticed to the right of our garden and in the direction of the view of hills, another cloud had formed immediately, as if out of thin air.

It stretched out part way towards the grey mist-like cloud, which was travelling from the opposite direction from the left-hand end of our garden as described above, whilst this new cloud formation was travelling in from the right-hand end of our garden to within about two-hundred feet or thereabouts of the first cloud formation.

I continued to watch and was astonished to observe strange flying vehicles and objects of all kinds, bathed in a golden yellow light with portals along the sides all lit up, coming out at the tip of the cloud nearest to the first lightning cloud. Thousands of them flew out of the cloud at fast speeds and disappeared some distance in the sky at the front of our house.

If you were to draw a line from the Northeast where the hills lay, towards the oak tree that was offset to the right of us, at the front of our house, Southwesterly, you would observe the flight path of these fantastic objects. I became very excited at this sighting because this event was strange and unparalleled anywhere else to my knowledge. I assumed that everyone who was standing there with me had observed the same events. However, it is not until many years later that I realised that they had not seen anything after the lightning had struck the ground.

In my excitement, I ran upstairs to my parent's bedroom to see if I could see where these strange craft were going, and looking out of the window, I observed them disappear a short distance away, between the lonely oak tree and the woods. The sky here was blue without a patch of cloud.

I never discussed this event with anyone after this, until recently, when in 1999, I watched the television channel four series *'Horizon'* programme, where it talked about storms and lightning strikes and in particular the earth-to-air strikes that had recently been observed by scientists.

As I watched these programmes I remembered my experiences from years before and noted the similarities. I discovered that a further and more peculiar reason for the study of storms is that the scientific faculty at NASA is very interested in what goes on at the top of storm clouds. It has apparently been observed from space, that objects have been seen, ascending and descending into these storm systems. I remembered my 'vision' of the strange crafts that flew out of the white cloud that formed opposite the lightning strike on a south-easterly/north-westerly line.

I also discovered that UFO's are frequently noted as using the same flight trajectory northeast to southwest as well as northwest to southeast, when observed from the ground. My interest grew in these channel-four programmes, so much, that I decided to videotape these programmes when next shown. As I was 'rewinding' one of the videotapes that I had recorded, I observed a strange metallic object descending into one of the storm systems viewed on the tape, an effect that was noted only when rewinding the film, but when played in normal mode, could not be seen apart from the storm itself. I now believe that this tape shows that UFO's and storm systems are synonymous with the phenomenon of UFO's and storm activity.

Once again, the evidence that there is something more to this world than we currently know of, convinces me that something, in my opinion, 'controls' and 'forms' the storm systems that we regularly experience throughout this world, (this possibility is also considered by Timothy Good, in his book *'Unearthly Disclosure'* where he states in his opening chapter, that the aliens have demonstrated their ability to control local weather systems (Good 2000, pages 23, 84 & 255), and which, in my opinion, produces these storms to manipulate the opening of 'other dimensions'.

In his chapter entitled *The Watchers: Protectors, Raiders, or Indifferent Observers,* Charles Berlitz, also suggests that: "Electromagnetic effects may provide a window or doorway to another dimension in time or space through which extraterrestrial beings may scientifically penetrate..." (Berlitz 1975, page 190).

Since that experience and others that I have related here, I have sought to understand something of the truth that lay behind my own personal experiences and why these should have happened to me.

Since those early encounters, I have begun to observe several related facts and Baal the storm-god is just one of these factors relating to this subject. The ancients worshipped Baal and he had a hermaphrodite form connection known as the Baalim and Asherim. Could this relationship with the Baalim and Asherim actually be two groups of alien beings that descended after the flood on mount Hermon? It is my opinion that a certain group of people who are in control of world events in history, actually know more about these things than we are led to believe. Baal worship still exists to day with a return to fire walking as well as bonfires and the increasing usage of fireworks throughout the year.

Reading of the Book of Enoch has enabled me to recognise certain aspects relating to the truth that has been hidden from the world at large, with regard to the fact that Aliens exist in our atmosphere. St Paul for example, speaks about his knowledge of the seventh and ninth heavens and Jesus speaks about his return to Earth in the last days and how he will come in clouds with great glory enveloped in a brilliant white light. How much more familiar can you get to the truth about aliens and UFO's and storm cloud systems, than this? The Bible makes use of the term *"Sons of Light"* to project similar imagery and the prophets always give similar descriptions of having observed bizarre visions of brilliant white lights, as bright as the sun or stars, prior to them receiving their prophecies. As well as being disturbed by this dazzling brilliance, their reports often feature beings shrouded in white light, or beings dressed in whiteness, who proceed to part with their instructions on human events. Aside from the very obvious connotations associated with the idea of 'white' in connection with purity, there is a sense in which these occurrences are literally self-contained light forces often with a mechanical physical presence such as have been described by observers of UFO phenomena in recent years.

These events also leave behind real physical yet unexplainable evidence such as imprints on the ground at landing sites or scorch marks on nearby trees and other plants or fauna. Often, these UFO encounters occur at times of intense periods of severe change. The book of Daniel is descriptive of this type of activity currently being under-played and trivialised by some modernist experts who it appears, believe in nothing but their own protestations, but they have witnessed nothing, or perceived anything of true value, scripturally how can they, for they are blind: "as it is written of them."

The prophet Isaiah, spoke of these elders and leaders of our world in a strong language describing them as those who have not known or understood the way that God intended they should, and therefore, "God hath shut their eyes, that they cannot see and their hearts that they cannot understand, nor are they capable of truly considering the effects of the things that they do and say". (KJV, Isaiah, chapter 44 v 17-20). These are, he says: "such that prefer to bow down to mounds and trees or to stones or sticks, the idols of their own abhorrent imaginings even today, for these walk in the lusts of their own inventions with their vain philosophies which cannot save them from utter damnation". These are, he says: "they, which are a blinding curse upon the nations having a form of Godliness yet whose purposes are to deceive the world", in an attempt to cheat God from his inheritance. Death and destruction follow their causes. Therefore, they continue to lie. These are they, who seek to suppress the truth in our society and will stop at nothing to achieve this. However, it is equally imperative that God also has a man with the ability to see, an enlightened visionary, knowing right and wrong, a vision of truth and light, of justice and mercy. The world has hope, but where is such a man today?

Furthermore, the Bible reveals that in the 'last days' (the days prior to the second Judgement foretold by Enoch), certain changes will take place that give us a clue to the 'end times' and these are frighteningly relevant to all of us who are living in these times of change. Enoch says: "that in those days a change shall take place..."

(Cited in: Charles 1997, page 68), and the second book of Timothy also states: "In the last days perilous times shall occur in which, men will be lovers of themselves, covetous, making false accusations about each other, despising those that are good and genuine" (2 Tim Ch 3 v 1). In the book of Romans a further definition of the end times is revealed in which the wrath of God is declared to be against all ungodliness and unrighteousness. "God has given mankind a reprobate mind to do these things, which they should not do" (Romans Ch 1 v 18-32).

"All these things must happen and then the end shall come", said Jesus to his disciples. This time is here, now! He also said, that we can discern the seasons. For example: "when we see a glorious sunset we know the day that is to come will be one of sunshine. Likewise, when the clouds are black and greyish and the winds are strong we know that a storm is brewing. You hypocrites you can discern the blatantly obvious yet you cannot discern the times in which you live" (Matthew 16 v 1-4), and how that judgement in righteousness will soon follow like a shadow on the wall or like a thief in the night. Enoch also states: "on the day of their affliction and anguish they shall not be able to save themselves" (Cited in: Charles 1997).

The world is constantly looking for peace but it is said that in the day they find it, shall come, 'sudden destruction', (Matthew 24 v 37). The world will never heed the voice of wisdom because it is rapt in its hedonistic ways and how can that which is fleshly partake of that which is spirit and life. One is visible and the other invisible.

How can someone, whose hedonistic way of life, based on love of the self and their own fleshly desires, even begin to accept the possibilities for the existence of spiritual beings yet alone perceive the existence of alien entities from outer or inner space? For example: the Bible has various stories which can be relative to our understanding of situations and experiences today. Take the story of that great prophet Elijah, who had gone to Mount Carmel to deride the prophets of Baal. When these prophets had built their altar of sacrifice to their false god Baal, they began dancing about and crying, and prophesying niceties to each other and some of them began cutting themselves in an effort to bring rain over the parched land, but nothing happened. This event took all day, when Elijah stepped into their midst, deriding them in front of the people of Israel. It was well into the evening and Elijah, standing alone with his servant in the midst of four hundred and fifty prophets of Baal, and four hundred prophets of the groves of Jezebel that ate at her table, began challenging the prophets of Baal to bring down fire from heaven. This he suggested they should do, if they thought that Baal was better than the Living God, to wit, Elijah built an altar and placed a sacrifice upon it. Then he got them to dowse it with water and dig a ditch round about the altar and fill it with water. When this was achieved, Elijah prayed to the living God who sent down fire from heaven in answer to Elijah's prayer. The fire consumed all the sacrifice, the altar, the water-filled ditch, and also the prophets of Baal that stood nearby mocking him. How is that for a statement of truth regarding the existence of the Living God?

During this same period, the prophet Elisha also experiences the revealed presence of a Living God, but further demonstrates the presence of *'the Watchers'* when Elisha's servant becomes terrified at the prospects of the presence of the king of Syria who came looking for Elisha. Unperturbed by this king, Elisha prays for his servant's eyes to be opened to the spiritual realm of God, in which he was able to see the host of heavenly watchers in the sky roundabout him. Elisha says to him: that "they *('the watchers')*, that are for us, are not against us", and the Lord God opened the young man's eyes so that he saw that the mountain was full of heavenly horses and chariots of fire, roundabout them. Now, just like Elisha's servant, I for one, would rather have the whole host of these heavenly beings on my side in a crisis, than any number of Earthly beings we call, mankind. However, the worship of false gods and the making of prayers to powers and principalities of the air, (to fallen angels, who also live in our atmosphere), is the main reason for the existence of God's judgement upon mankind. For which reason also, due to original sin, this same judgement has been determined over seventy generations, according to Enoch, totalling 25,480 years in all and which, will come to an abrupt end in the last days. This reference to the 'last days' is not only recorded by Enoch and all the prophets as well as the Bible, but can be found in many other ancient sources such as the Mayan Prophecies, The red Indian tribes of north America, the Dalai Llama and other similar beliefs that have this common theme contained in them, and which, are just too complex and too numerous to mention in detail here. My primary concern is with the revelations about alien existence and their possible connection with angels, but it is well to note, that according to the book of Enoch: "In the last days, these Angels shall once more descend and abduct all those who are the children of sin and gather them together into the holding places. Then shall the execution of Judgement be amongst the sinners, but over the righteous and holy however, he shall appoint guardian angels from among the holy watchers" (Cited in: Charles 1997, page 143). It becomes even more evident, when we put these biblical elements into the wider perspective concerning aliens and UFO's that these themes contain much more than simple religious dogma.

"... And it shall come to pass
in those days *(the last days)*
that the Elect and Holy Children
will descend from the high heaven,
and their seed will become one
with the children of men".

(The Book of Enoch: xxxix; page 57).

CHAPTER EIGHT

Vision of a Brilliant White Light over Stoney-Cross

Returning home one Sunday evening from an outing with my family, we were travelling through Stoney Cross, an old airfield situated in the New Forest. After a short distance my father suddenly pulled over to the side of the road. He appeared to be concerned about something on, or near the road, slightly ahead of us. He decided to get out and take a proper look and my mother did likewise.

Curious about what could be happening, I decided to do the same and as I did so I saw that several vehicles had also stopped and a small group of people, about twenty observers in all, were standing nearby, transfixed by some strange phenomena going on a short distance up the road ahead of us. I too became fascinated at what I was witnessing as I caught sight of a large white object hovering above.

It is hard to describe, concerning the nature of this object, as it was shrouded in a brilliant white light. However, the object hovered in the air some forty to fifty feet above ground level. It was a magnificent star-like globe that floated from side to side of the road, somewhat erratically, as if attempting to stabilise itself. This display of luminosity continued for a while, seemingly unaware of our presence, but as we watched in awe of this sighting, the star-like giant, hovering above the roadway, began disappearing momentarily, and then reappearing again, which it repeated several times throughout our observations. This disappearing act was considered by some as an indication of its awareness of us all standing there a short distance from it. Following this strange disappearing and re-appearing act, the object also expanded and contracted in size to the amazement of all the onlookers. This star-like brilliance did the whole act repeatedly for several minutes. Then suddenly, it began to climb at a sharp angle towards our left, at which point I heard a rushing sound similar to that of the harrier jump jet I had observed taking off a few years earlier (as described in a previous chapter), and with that, the star-like luminosity, as big as a house, took off at great speed into space. From where I was standing, I observed that it looked just like any other star hanging there in the blackness of the night.

Convinced that the show was finally over, the small crowd began to dissipate and eventually we did the same. No one discussed this event, which I thought was very strange to say the least. However, like all the other events I have witnessed so far, I never forgot it. My search for an explanation has taken me to many avenues of thought over the years in search of the truth. How is it that a star can move out of its place in the heavens and come to Earth, like this one did and return the same way?

The answer to this question is also found in the book of Enoch, where he reveals his knowledge concerning the problems of sin throughout the universe being caused by the stars that transgress their order. The bible also deals with this subject in a more closed manner. These stars are said to fall to Earth and indicate the beginnings of judgement (Matt.24v29) & (Mark 13v24). So, we can see from this, that stars do not always stay in their courses. We can also see that there are those who have some knowledge of these stars' capabilities to move about at will, and to behave in a paranormal fashion. This includes stars or meteors falling to Earth in a controlled manner and not necessarily crashing to Earth, as the scientific and governmental academies would have us believe, though this is equally possible and which, could be a symptomatic explanation for the American Roswell incidence of 1947 and the Welsh UFO incident in 1996.

Enoch himself speaks of these stars, which can even, collide together and change their form forever, possibly even increasing in size and then like lightning, explode, filling the nearby universe with brilliance and star-debris, which form the nucleus of new stars. The stars that fail to keep their order are the primary cause of universal chaos, threatening the very foundation of the universe, including our planet.

This is the revelation of Enoch that is only part of a wider picture presented in the Enochian fragments. Like Enoch, what I witnessed that night on Stoney Cross, was a revelation that we are truly living in the last days spoken of by the prophets of old and by the early church elders, Apostles and Jesus, who himself, also referred to these events many times in the Gospels.

The author Robert Temple, writes in his book, *The Sirius Mystery*, and I quote: "what is the hypothesis, then, which has been so startlingly confirmed in the best traditions of science?" (Temple 1998, page 4). This he stated, concerning his determination to show that a group of people known as the Dogon had hidden, in their secret rituals, evidence of a second and third star contained within the Sirius System (Temple 1998, Ch. 2, *The Knowledge of the Dogon*).

Scientists ridiculed Temple when he claimed for over twenty years, that Sirius C was a red dwarf star. Science could not find it and dismissed Temple as a crank. Yet recently he has been confirmed as being correct. Sirius C exists! Yet, what are the concluding efforts of Temple on this issue, and the driving force for his book, it is this: that our planet has at sometime in the past been visited by intelligent beings from the system of the star Sirius" (Temple 1998).

Sirius is approximately eight light years away from Earth and is our closest neighbour as far as stars are concerned. It is interesting to note that the movements of the sun, stars and the moon all have an effect on our planet especially Earth's climates.

In 1976, I was standing on Bournemouth Promenade with some friends discussing the greatness of God and the good mercy of Jesus Christ in providing the only version of salvation for mankind anywhere in the world. More specifically, we were discussing a Biblical quotation, which states: "that there is no other name given under heaven whereby we must be saved except the name Jesus Christ". In the process of our discourse, I was impressed with a message that 'God' would prove himself that day forward by changing the times and the seasons from this moment onwards. Uncertain of this statement at this time, I was to discover it in the book of Daniel, at a point where Nebuchadnezzar recounts his dream to the young man and where he states that a watcher, a holy one, came down from heaven and cried: "Hew down the tree and cut off the branches, shake off the leaves and scatter the fruit" (Daniel, Ch 4 v 13). Daniel informs the king that this matter is by a decree of the watchers themselves to the intent that: "the living may know that the most high rules over the kingdoms of men" and where he also says, that it is the lord who raises or deposes Kings and alters the times and seasons according to his purposes.

Twenty years later, I heard a meteorologist exclaim that for the past twenty years since 1976, the seasons had predominantly changed and that it was continuing to do so. According to this man, we had apparently suffered a reduction in the seasons owing to global changes that have resulted in only two distinctive seasons, namely summer and winter.

Whereas I was able to reconcile this event of the past twenty years or so to an act of God, who incidentally told me to tell those listening at the time that this would happen as proof that God is God and that there is none other, and that it is 'He' who controls the affairs of men. The Meteorologist claimed his knowledge was based on a change in the system of global warming. Just what is that exactly? Surely, global warming is none other than a direct effect of something instituted by a direct act of the Living God, who said it would be like this, way back in the Bible some 5000 years ago, and again in 1976 AD, on a Bournemouth promenade. Yet, despite this connection to the climate of change going on in our world, still men will not believe in the living God or the fact that they are answerable for their actions against God. So why should they believe in stars that move across the sky and those, that countless observers have seen moving from star to star? Why should the millions of testimonies of individuals, or the many group observations, of flying saucers, UFO's, and alien abductions, involving mainly female abductees, as reported in the book of Enoch and the Bible, the British press since the late 1940's, and specialised or niche magazines, be any different? Why should they believe it, indeed? Is it because this type of detailed information conflicts with their self-indulgent interests and their richly guarded hedonistic lifestyles, as well as the opportunity to make money whilst the sun is shining? Unfortunately, those who put their trust in riches cannot enter the kingdom of God. Can it be that the world is afraid to admit this knowledge to itself for fear of panic? Who knows what the reasons for non-disclosure really are!

The fact is, that as stated in the first chapter of this work, humanity is continuously observing strange and varied phenomena involving aliens and UFO's, for which we can have no positive rational explanation whatsoever, despite our scientific or religious opinions.

Is it any less true then, concerning the Enochian fragments in which, it also recorded that the fate and judgement imposed on Azazael and Semjaza, (the two angel beings who descended on mount Hermon, in the days of Jared), was horrific. They were caught by the men of those times, and held in Abel's Jail according to Enoch. Eventually, sentence was passed upon them by the Lord of Spirits, that they should be bound hand and foot and cast into a dark pit and jagged rocks placed over Azazael, whilst Semjaza and the 120 who were with them, were to be cast into deep ravines or valleys for seventy generations, after which, the judgement of God would come upon the entire world. This judgement, according to all prophetic works is soon to come upon us.

Enoch says that in the 'last days', in the days of the book of revelations mentioned in the Bible, that fire will fall from heaven and consume all the sinners. When will this event occur? Enoch says that in the days when: "Iron, Copper Silver, Gold, Aluminium and Steel" shall lose their value and be of no more practical use. "No man will be able to buy or sell, for bronze will no longer be of service and tin shall have no use; and lead shall be done away with".

These last days that are referred to shall be an exact mirror of the days in which the first judgement of mankind appeared and are said to be the same as the days of Noah mentioned in the Bible, in particular, the book of revelations, which describes this mirroring as a common market period such as, the 'treaty of Rome'. During this period, the day will come when we will not be able to buy or sell anything unless we have the 'Mark of the beast'. At the same time, this 'Mark' is a cosmetic issue possibly linked in someway to British Telecom's 'Eye Catcher 2000' project and developed in some form of microchip product inserted into the hand or forehead, which could then be read by computers using some kind of barcode technology. If these 'last days' are not the same days recorded in the many prophetical works I have alluded to, then what days are these? The sign of such 'days' are the ones in which a ram and a goat do battle, (see chapters 12 & 13 for more explanation of this). Furthermore, this same period is the days in which the watchers of heaven, the angels of God, are said to return. If the words of Enoch are true then I believe these are the days he has described.

CHAPTER NINE

Opening of Windows in Heaven

Then Elisha said: "Hear ye the word of the Lord; thus saith the lord, tomorrow about this time shall a measure of fine flour be sold for a shekel, and two measures of Barley for a shekel, in the gate of Samaria. Then a Nobleman on whose hand the King was leaning answered and said: Behold, if the Lord would make windows in Heaven, might this thing be? And Elisha answered and said: you behold, for thou shalt see it with thine eyes, but shall not partake of it" (2 Kings Ch.7 v 2).

And so it came to pass, which Elisha spoke to the people, and the Nobleman witnessed the same words come to pass the next day and met his fate as prophesied, for the people trod upon him in the gate of Samaria, and he died, (2 Kings Ch.7 v19).

And it shall come to pass also, that he who fleeth from the noise of the fear shall fall into the pit; and he that cometh up out of the midst of the pit shall be taken by the snare: for the Windows from on high are open, and the foundations of the Earth do shake, (Isaiah Ch.24 v18). "Bring ye all the tithes into the storehouse, that there may be meat in mine house, and prove me now herewith, saith the Lord of Hosts, and see if I will not open you the windows of Heaven, and pour you out a blessing, that there shall not be room enough to receive it" (Malachi Ch.3 v10).

Mirrors are a well-known allegory for referencing the patterns of 'Heaven on Earth'. Those who have understanding of this can identify the reflections of Earthly patterns mirrored by heaven as well as the heavenly ones mirrored by Earth. To the untrained or uninitiated, these patterns shall be forever invisible to them. Unbelievers shall never know them although they traverse them all the days of their lives.

Yet, for those who see the patterns of all things past and present, both in the stars and on the Earth, they shall read them and know them and so shall they live by them for they are footstool and throne of the Lord of Hosts, the true King of heaven. For where the heart is there shall thy treasures also be (Matthew 6 v 21).

Enoch also supports this biblical statement. He wrote, in his opening chapter, that the Holy One: "will come forth from his dwelling place, and that the eternal God will tread upon the Earth, even upon Mount Sinai, and appear from his camping place, and appear in the strength of His might from the heaven of heavens". Furthermore, Enoch also states: "that all shall be smitten with fear, and even the Watchers shall quake…"

It is interesting to note that these same feelings of fear and trembling also accompanied the young lads I wrote about in chapter three. Without a doubt these feelings were experienced when they attempted to relay to those of us who remained in the woods that day, that they had been 'terrorised' by an orange, pulsating globe. This globe appeared threatening to them because it would not allow them to leave the woods and head for home.

Since 1947, numerous stories have been handed down to the present day regarding many similar encounters with UFO's and strange beings from outer space. The same feelings of fear and trembling accompanied these encounters and visitations reported from around the world. Yet, many governments remain silent about these issues. Why is this?

According to some researchers, both American, British and Russian government agencies are spending billions of dollars on studying ancient manuscripts including the Bible and the Koran. They are also spending money on the Giza Pyramids, and in particular, the area of the Sphinx, which in 1992, was discovered to have hidden vaults, deep underground and are said to contain the 'book of Toth'. These same governments apparently had plans to be present at a secret opening of these vaults in or around the year's 2000/2001, which may or may not have occurred on this occasion. Why this special interest at this time? Is there a connection between the two events? Is this an ongoing SETI enhanced project in the search for ET?

The search for knowledge of the past and the search for knowledge of the stars above, do seem to be tied to a search for ET.

What is the connection? Is it, that mankind is about to be told, that aliens visited the Earth: not only around 5,000 years ago as Temple believes, but as far back as 22,000 years BC.

What is more compelling for me, is that this event occurred in the days of Jared, which was subsequently recorded in the books of Enoch, and by Noah, who in turn carried these books across the floods in his ark. Later, these books were handed down to future generations, in the hope that the truth will one day be told to the world.

Just what is that truth? Is it, that original sin most handsomely attributed to humanity alone, is not, primarily, the fault of humans, but the fault of a handful of lustful, fallen Angels, from the camp of Lucifer? Angels, who, for no other apparent reasons, other than that of apparent jealousy, sexual deviance and pleasure, crossed the boundaries of time and space to commit this deed against the human race.

These Angels, knowing that their actions would have dire consequences for mankind, bound themselves by mutual imprecations, to transgress the order of the universe and the 'Law' of God. In so doing, they knew that their actions would bring humankind into a place of unwitting disservice to a holy and vengeful God, ultimately leading to the fall of man. Is this the secret behind the biblical message and the real reason why God has made a propitiatory remedy through the sacrifice of his son, to rectify what the watchers of heaven have done to mankind? If so, then who has tampered with the scriptures to delay or remove the evidence of this from the early chapters; is it an attempt to hide this truth from us, and why? What other possible reasons could there be for doing so in the first place, unless someone, or some families, of someone, is awaiting a return of these beings at some future date. The Bible does appear to indicate a feudal battle between two specific Patriarchal lineages, namely the camp of God and Jesus Christ and the camp of Satan and as yet the 'man' whose name is a number (666), (Revelations Ch.13 v11-18) not yet revealed to the nations, but who, in my opinion bears the name John or Mark as in (John-Mark), the one who would sit with his head on Jesus. This is the connection with John, who I believe is the real Judas that betrayed Jesus, and who may be the 'dark lord' also referred to in Tolkien's Trilogy, *'The Lord of the Rings'*, summed up by the poetry chanted throughout the story as follows: "Three rings for the elven *(eleven)* Kings under the sky, Seven rings for the Dwarf-Lords in their halls of stone, Nine for mortal men doomed to die, One for the 'Dark Lord' on his dark throne… One ring to rule them all, one ring to find them, One ring to bring them all and in the darkness bind them…"

If this man, the dragon, the beast of Revelations, does not yet exist, could this being be a product of hybridisation? A being, genetically engineered by the aliens perhaps, who are also said to be responsible for the animal mutilation stories concerning the surgical removal of animal body parts and tissue samples. Is it possible that such a person exists? Could this person be placed among us waiting for the day of recognition as the world's long awaited problem solver, a highly skilled wizard/magician, secretly supported by a league of ten nations, with familiar links dating back to prehistoric times, stemming from a link with the alien leaders that landed on mount Hermon in the days of Jared?

These angelic beings traded in magic rites and other skills for the favour of women. It is interesting to note that such a street wizard does exist already and who may be a forerunner of this being that is to come, and who currently goes by the name of David.

If this is feasible, then there is some logic to the conspiracy theories currently abounding the twenty-first century. Indeed, it would be true to say that this group of people, if they exist, would want to control the course of history and inevitably, if possible, change it to suit their purposes. In fact, when you compare this knowledge with the writings in the Scriptures, you can get a comparison of why God is continually re-affirming and re-establishing His purposes, in the order of things.

Reading the works and sayings of His chosen prophets, clearly indicates this analogy throughout all of the Old, and even the New Testament. The Bible deals with the fall of man as a tragic consequence of sin caused initially by Satan and his angels, but because of this act of sin, God sets about, through a series of divine interventions, to bring about a means of restoration for mankind and ultimately salvation.

The world of course has failed to understand this pattern of events and the reason is, because the truth surrounding the origin of sin has been cleverly altered and therefore, those responsible have instead, turned a valid relationship between God and Man into a religion of sorts, which of course, it is clearly not, for the sole purpose of controlling nations. Somehow, humanity has been caught up in a universal conspiracy contrived initially by a group of alien beings from heaven to conduct their own affairs on an unbeknown and gullible human race.

This group of beings, known in the Book of Enoch as the 'Satan's', and referred to as 'the Daemons' by the Medieval Nations of Europe, have also been currently referred to, by the modern Americans, as 'the Greys'. How is it possible then, that we can continue to promote the belief that mankind is alone in this universe, when there are thousands of recorded sightings of strange beings, and other similarly related phenomena, being clearly labelled by large groups of people, within differing social backgrounds, throughout history. This phenomenon, often involving peculiar-looking humanoid type beings with strange magical powers and abilities, has persisted for thousands of years to the present day, and which, cannot be solely the by-product of our own vain imaginings. Surely therefore, this is a secret that has been kept hidden from the developing world. Is this the 'secret' that world Governments are currently covering up?

Thankfully, there are a number of different groups of thinkers, dissidents, conspiracy theorists, and ufologists etcetera, who are at least, trying to persuade governments, to part with the evidence of this kind.

Many researchers are lobbying congress groups, and ministers are being constantly questioned about events happening in British and foreign skies; and although there is no definitive denial of the existence of these events, there is no admonishing of them either. If the presence of alien forces are at work in our atmosphere and governments are covering up this evidence could it be, that these forces are really hostile to us?

In an interview with Timothy Good, Kelly Cahill suggests, what many of us have also considered to be the case "that some of these alien entities are more interested in our 'souls' or our 'life-force' than our bodies and manipulating things that we are still debating the existence of and this she says, may be why we cannot understand the reasons for the abduction phenomenon not just because they are interested in our biological make-up and cultures, but also because of our spiritual make-up too, they have to approach us in different ways" (Cited in: Good 2000, page 55). If this is true, then the Enochian fragments are well justified in warning the world of the existence of these beings and their relationship to God and an impending final judgement upon mankind, because these issues that I am writing about are spiritual matters and because these beings are also operating on a spiritual level too because they are spiritual beings, Angels of Light or Angels of Darkness. My personal opinion is that these aliens are utilizing human DNA in the form of 'genetic pollination' in some way and may actually be involved in human ancestry of which, patriarchal ancestry tracing is only a reflection of our ancient past and this may also be true, if God is our Father.

CHAPTER TEN

A Vision of a Heavenly Chariot

The estate where I grew up had become a difficult area to live in. It was as if something demonic was happening in that place. The young people I grew up with had somehow changed too. They had grouped themselves together in mischievous fashion and were frequently becoming disruptive to the locals as they began behaving like vandals, (Incidentally this is an interesting word to use especially since in Roman times it was a warring group called *Vandals* that raided Rome around circa 400-435 AD.).

Some of the teenagers on the estate had ended up in court eventually, as a result of their petty criminal activities, and partly due also to the number of complaints that were made to the local police from those affected by the unsocial behaviour of these youths. Nevertheless, many of these complaints were met with a lack of support from the police, (this lack of police involvement has become an increasingly popular story around the country in recent years too, as lack of resources and political will to control criminal behaviours, makes policing impossible). It was evident, that the police clearly knew those responsible for the aggressive environment in which the estate was now accustomed, but preferred to turn a 'blind eye' to the situation or, were simply powerless to stop it.

Several families had witnessed what seemed like an endless nightmare for the locals, who found themselves victims of those who sought to perpetrate their aggressive challenging behaviours against anyone who dared to stand up to them.

How did it come to be like this? What caused these dramatic changes in the local community?

Shortly after this period, I had a dream in which, I saw a road well worn with time. This road came to a fork, in which a signpost stood, showing a way to the left and a way to the right, clearly a decision had to be made here. Which way must I go? Left or right?

In my dream however, I suddenly found that I had taken the left fork. The reason for this appeared to be the statement: "The obvious is very seldom true."

It was also apparent to me in my dream, as I stood pondering the way ahead, that most people would choose the road to the right, since this was the clearer and more obviously used route. Initially, it was at first my choice also. However, I felt compelled to take the left fork and soon after, I began walking along it.

Soon, I began to notice that the path I was walking along had become a narrow track, something like a rabbit run, and which stretched out before me into a wild expanse and by now, the track appeared to be in the middle of some desert place.

It was at this point, armed with my self-doubts, that I began to be afraid, (something that most of us experience at some time or other in our lives). Where was I? What was this strange place? This was unfamiliar territory and how did I really get there in the first place? Looking around me, I wondered if I had done the right thing choosing this path and I began to argue with myself because I felt compelled to be here and not by my own choosing. Then suddenly, I heard a voice saying: "Fear not! It will come **'right'** in the end!" and immediately after I heard this voice, I found myself walking this very sketchy pathway out into this unknown desert place where I continued to feel totally isolated. That is when I awoke, sweating and shaking all over.

Nevertheless, deep inside me, I felt instinctively that I knew the meaning of this dream, for as always, God gives the interpretation where there is no interpreter to assist and this was a strange dream indeed. Years later, I began to re-discover the meaning of this dream in my life. Much later still, I finally realise that the things that have happened to me, could not have become part of my own personal experience, without my behaving in such a way that would enable me to both see and hear the things that 'He' chose to show to me.

This understanding that I am acquiring, is clearly *solis sacerdotibus* to those whom the Living God initiates into the inner sanctum of his purposes and what a privilege that God should do this to anyone! What is more, the revelation that 'He' never does anything, without first revealing his intentions to someone of his choosing, even though He may not have yet revealed the exact nature or purpose of his choice as this may depend on our responses to His guidance and whether we are open to His leadings.

Some time after this event, I experienced another strange vision, one in which I was wide awake, having my eyes wide open, and this vision still leaves me with a feeling of awe approximately, some thirty years later.

It was the year 1976, and once again it was a warm and sunny summer's weekend. At about the evening time, just as the sun was descending on its Southwesterly course, I had this compulsion to go outside to my father's car, apparently to retrieve something from it. As I approached the car I looked up toward the sky, as I often do, when I saw what appeared to be a square, opening in the sky above me and to my right.

It was as if someone was sliding back a portion of the sky, just like on a commercial freezer door. I could see a deeper blue within, which reached to darkness beyond. Then suddenly, in the same instance, a strange craft flew through this 'window' and drew level with me as I approached the car.

Once again, this event occurred over the field that I have described several times before in previous chapters. As you know, the front of the house we lived in looked out onto a road that ran approximately south to southwest and our house faced approximately southwest. The field opposite our house was 'L-shaped' towards the village and stretched out below us.

This view through the village was partially obscured by a very tall, ancient oak tree that stood alone in the dip of the field, (also described earlier), and which was connected by a footpath that ran down to the main road of the village from our estate. This footpath passed right alongside the oak tree, which could be touched as people went by, it was that close. Despite the many changes that have transformed this area, this tree still stands there today, and I hope, for many years to come. (For me, it is the only remaining physical evidence of the things that I am relating to you, the reader).

Having stepped out of the front door of our house and turning right angles from the doorstep, I began to walk down the path to the road. As I scanned the view over the field opposite me, my eyes caught a glimpse of an opening in the sky to my right and above me, when I was instantly confronted by a large spacecraft descending through this 'window', glowing red with heat, which indicated to me that it had passed through our atmosphere. I watched in amazement as it quickly dropped down in front of the large oak tree, slightly offset to my right ahead of me, where it came to an abrupt halt approximately 35 - 45 feet above the ground where it cooled itself immediately. The spacecraft stood there in the air, floating, and jet-black. As I continued to watch the craft, it moved slowly across my field of vision and slightly to my left. I noted that it was somewhat bell-shaped with a bauble-like thing on top of it, almost like the pole of a tent.

Another peculiarity, I also observed, was that it was hexagonal in shape and very pronounced at the base. This craft was also slatted and had tanks and communication equipment attached to the outside of it and the windows were slatted making it look like some sort of scout ship, or reconnaissance device. Naturally, I cannot be certain of its type, because I have never seen anything like this object before in my entire life.

Underneath the craft, I observed another strange and peculiar thing. In the centre of the craft's underside there was a hole surrounded by a thick and heavy structure of metalwork, which was salient to the base and circular, with another metal fixture in between. Inside the hole itself, I observed flames and heat. The rest of the base was of shiny, silvery metal plates with a swirled pattern effect, as the plates lay flat against each other, very smooth, and which moved independently but created openings like the swirled shutters of an electric fan. The flooring seemed to be comprised of a series of peculiar shaped plates that slid over, or under each other, to create various swirling patterns, (might this craft be the type that produces the swirled effects noted in, and associated with, the crop circle phenomenon, and might this craft be a link to these patterns)? As these plates moved around and opened and shut in various swirled patterns it was as if the floor was alive!

The outer housing of the craft that sat above the flooring and the base, also spun around independently in anti-clockwise motion to the floor and had at its edging, a massive ring with a series of inner rings going up inside it, to meet the flooring. These were all dotted underside with spaced bolts or holes in a different metal and colour. There was so much to take in within the few minutes of the sighting. The overall appearance of the craft was that it was wide at the base and tapered upwards to the top and looked predominantly like a fifty-pence piece as it slowly rotated around. It remained motionless in the air all the time I was observing it.

Whilst I was witnessing this event unfolding before my very eyes, I realised that no one else appeared to have seen it or even come out to look at it; and by now, I was uncertain of how to behave in front of this thing as it hovered, about forty feet or so from where I stood. So, bending down on one knee I reached for a pebble from the garden, and standing again I began to shout, hoping that someone would come and see what I was seeing, and as I did so, I threw the pebble to see if it could hit the spacecraft. The reason was two-fold. Firstly, to check if this was real and not imaginary. Secondly, to gauge something of the distance of it from where I was standing.

I became afraid and shouted loudly for someone to come and look and eventually my father emerged at the front doorway asking me what the commotion was about.

I pointed at the silent craft, which was now moving slowly away to my left out over the front of the estate and the main road that ran through the centre of the village, and up the hill. From our front door, you could easily see the hill as it ran south of the road.

This was undoubtedly a UFO that I observed and it was as big as a house and it disappeared over the hillside approximately 1.5 miles away. Pointing towards the spacecraft, I asked my father if he saw it. His response was not very clear as I followed him indoors trying to ascertain his feelings about the UFO sighting and once again, he did not engage in conversation about this and we never spoke of this afterwards. Stranger still, was the fact that no reports of this particular daylight sighting was ever made by anyone travelling through our village or by anyone travelling down the hill towards the West Country, or from anyone living in the street where this incident occurred.

If any reports were made, these were clearly dismissed or covered up. Most peculiar indeed, because the view from the hill is amazing, as you can see everything for several miles above and across the village and its woodlands in the distance beyond. By my calculations, anything that stood thirty feet or more above the ground would be clearly sighted from the hilltop.

None could dismiss this sighting easily for several reasons. Firstly, It was in broad daylight and in full sunshine. Secondly, It was as big as a house and it was black, and thirdly, it was not in a hurry to disappear, as its pace was slow and controlled. It went over the hill and in my opinion it landed there.

I never saw it again, but then I was deeply concerned about this too because I could not explain its presence in the first place, at least not at that time. After many years had passed and on reflection, I asked my father if he could remember that incident and if he could tell me what he saw. He replied that he could remember that day but that by the time he got to the front doorstep he did not really see anything.

It was then that I realised, like so many others who have experienced similar UFO encounters with alien spacecraft, that I stood alone. Who will ever believe this story? If those closer to me will not believe the experiences I have related to them, even when some of them have boasted of their own paranormal experiences in the past, then who else would believe me?

I never sought the help of the establishment on this sighting or my other experiences because I was afraid that I would be rubbished, or discredited in some way, and this was far more scarier than the actual sighting itself, so I decided to keep this to myself.

As time passed, more people were beginning to experience this phenomenon and to debate UFO's and numerous other sightings that were becoming more widely observed; and through better reporting of this phenomenon, the stories began to be relayed in newspapers and when they did, I would reveal little by little, some of my own experiences of that day in 1976. Having told friends and colleagues, I was mocked and frowned upon by those who were clearly disturbed by my tale, but I have never let this behaviour deter me from searching for answers to this enigma.

CHAPTER ELEVEN

The trouble with Angels

People only believe what they can see with their own eyes. It does not matter what individual people may have experienced themselves, they will not be believed.

Yet often, on the other hand, people can be so gullible that they will believe just about anything. So you see, if you tell a story that does not go beyond the extraordinary day to day things you actually stand a better chance of being believed than if you happen to tell of something true, but so intriguing, that it is beyond belief.

Now this tale of Enoch's is just such a tale that is easily dismissed as being beyond belief. Enoch overhears Michael the Archangel speaking to a fellow angel named Raphael, in which they discuss the concept of judgement cast upon the fallen angels at Mount Hermon. In the process of this discussion, Michael considers the horrors of such a judgement pronounced on the fallen angels and also the effects of this same judgement being placed upon the human race as well. According to Enoch, It came to pass whilst they both stood before the Lord of Spirits, that Michael turned to Raphael and said: "I would not take their part under the eye of the Lord of Spirits, for this seems to be the reason for the Lord's angry response to them, because they have behaved as if they were the Lord." Enoch continues with his description of the names of some of the heavenly perpetrators. Their names are as follows:

The first of them was Semjaza (mentioned in a previous chapter). The second was named Artaqifa. The third was called Armen. The fourth was called Kokabel. The fifth was named Turael. The sixth Rumjal. The seventh Danjal. The eighth was called Neqael. The ninth was Baraqel. The tenth was called Azazel. The eleventh was named Armaros. The twelfth named Batarjal. The thirteenth called Busasejal. The fourteenth called Hananel. The fifteenth was named Turel and the sixteenth Simapesiel. The seventeenth was Jetrel and the eighteenth was called Tumael. The nineteenth was named Turel and the twentieth called Rumael whilst the twenty-first was named Azazel, these are the names of those angels that Enoch reports as being responsible for acts against creation, the human race, and more importantly against the Living God.

The list below, are of the names of the angel leaders, who caused their minions to commit acts of gross indecency with the daughters of men and these are as follows:

The first was Jeqon. He was initially responsible for leading astray the sons of God, and actively encouraging them to descend to the Earth, from the heavens, and to have sexual relations with the daughters of men. The second angel leader was called Asbeel and he was in league with Jeqon to provide evil counsel and powers of persuasion to actually carry out acts of indecency with the women of Earth. The third angel being was called Gadreel and it is clear from Enoch's writings that Gadreel had visited the Earth previously for it was Gadreel that came and led Eve astray having showed to her and all mankind the death blows and also the weapons of death and destruction to the sons of men. He introduced humanity to the art of warfare and showed them how to make shields and spears and also the coats of mail as well as the art of sword making. From his hand, men have learned the art of battle and this is the primary cause of death in the world.

The Bible speaks of the downfall of humankind because of the deception of Eve with a serpent angel whom Enoch identifies as Gadreel. How much more proof do we need to realise that there are 'Forces' at work in the world even today, who are under the influence of serpent angel beings from another world. Hard to believe, especially when the American government spends billions of dollars every year persuading Hollywood directors to produce films showing serpent beings wreaking havoc on the world and committing heinous crimes against the innocents. A mass of people who are easily hypnotised into believing that this phenomenon is all in the mind, or as the Bible cleverly puts it, "Having their consciences seared with a hot iron." What more cleverly contrived hot iron can you get than cinema, video or television, for searing the consciences of the people more than this? 'Serpent beings' descending from heaven to Earth no way, not ever, except in comics or the big screen or television. So, why does Enoch tell his story like this? For example, why does Enoch reveal their names such as

Gadreel? Gadreel is the one noted by Enoch as that darling serpent of Eve, the mother of mankind, who was led astray by this serpent being? The Bible claims he was the subtlest of all beasts of the field. Or, why do the Hindu people of India for example, tell stories of the gods who flew about in vimanas, (flying cars), throwing bolts of lightning at each other, with some kind of atomic laser or 'lightning weapon'? If these stories have no truth in them therefore, then who is fooling whom?

It does not end there however, the fourth angel being was called Penemue and he, in my opinion, is Toth of the Egyptians. He was the one who taught writing and the secrets of wisdom, science and mathematics and herbal medicine. He was the one who instructed mankind in writing with pen and paper and as a result of this method, mankind, coupled with their newfound knowledge of warfare, were taught by their serpent mentors from beyond the stars, to continue in their sinful ways from eternity to eternity. For, writes Enoch: "men were not created for such a purpose as this to give confirmation of their faith with pen and ink. For men were created to be just like the angels themselves, continuing in righteousness, so that death would not have taken hold of mankind". This knowledge of death and the ways of death has caused mankind to perish in the judgement flood.

The fifth angel was called Kasdeja and he taught men the secrets of wicked smiting or witchcraft, Smitings of the Spirits and smitings of the embryo in the womb, as well as the bites of serpents, and the smitings of the soul, (as found in Caribbean countries and known as Voodoo). Therefore, whoever these angelic beings are, they are responsible for the destruction and degradation and suffering experienced in our world, even today.

The Bible warns us that as in the days of Noah: "so shall it be in those days when the son of man cometh." This is a prophecy concerning men's interest in witchcraft and the magic circle that the world finds fascinating and which will increase in the last days alongside man's need for warfare, terrorism, genetic engineering, euthanasia and increasing violent crime.

The enigmas that currently surround the UFO and abduction phenomenon are not new. The medieval stories and past folklore all indicate similar patterns of behaviour within the mythological/paranormal subject core. Therefore, we can be certain that what we are witnessing today, occurred with the same degree of frequency prior to the days of Enoch's father, Jared. Man's desire for spiritual enlightenment and restitution with God's holy presence opened the windows of heaven for all kinds of bizarre principalities to enter Earth's atmosphere and seek to dwell among us. In so doing the authority of God was also challenged, and the result was a primary cause of first judgement upon mankind, which occurred in the days of Noah (The Flood, circa 23824 - 23823).

The Bible informs us that in the last days of reckoning, (the days of Noah), as indicated also by Enoch, that a similar awakening will herald the final judgement of mankind, which will most certainly take place. As the song says: 'Que Serah, Serah, whatever will be, will be. The futures not ours to see...' or is it? According to Enoch, the future ends with alien contact and an act of final judgement being fulfilled after seventy generations have happened. Should this information continue to be kept hidden from the public domain? Surely, everyone has the right to know the fate that awaits him or her in the future? A fate that not only ends in death, because the Bible says: "there is a way which seems right to a man but the end of these ways are the ways of death" (Proverbs Ch.14 v 12), but also ends in a second death, (which suggests that not only can you 'live twice' i.e.: being *'born'* and then spiritually being *'born again'* (John Ch.3 v 3)), but that you can, (if life takes you this way), taste death twice, (Revelations Ch.2 v 11). Firstly, having gone through the natural or fatalistic causes of death and secondly, through being cast into outer darkness where there shall be gnashing of teeth, (i.e. Hell), a result of the second judgement being cast on the world as foretold by Enoch and others, including Jesus.

CHAPTER TWELVE

My quest for an answer to some of the enigmas begins

I believe that things happen for a purpose, at least to some of us, if not to everyone, though I did not know this at the time, but I have learned it since. It appears that circumstances make life changes for us, sometimes for the better and sometimes for our chastening. Hard lessons for anyone to learn, especially lessons such as this: "That, he whom the Lord loves, He chastens; be zealous therefore and repent" (Revelations Ch.3 v 19).

When other people appear to get involved in a person's life, things that take place are not all sweetness and light. However, when God intervenes in someone's life you can be sure that there will be moments of sadness and sorrow as well as moments of great joy and comfort that only the Living God, as 'Father' gives, but this knowledge can only be understood or experienced by someone, attempting to get closer to God, and can only be found by those who are willing to make a real effort in their zeal for God through repentance and obedience to his will. Through such obedient closeness we can discover the real secrets of spiritual revelation.

In this state, the true believer should be able to experience the unexplained things that all the prophets of old experienced, and which the apostles of the early church also experienced. It is in this state of being, that I too therefore, also believe that I had these selfsame experiences and that they were not of my making and neither could I rationalise them when they occurred, no matter how hard I tried.

My quest for personal understanding of the UFO enigma, relating to my own experiences, had briefly introduced me to someone with similar interests in the paranormal. This occurred back in 1982, during which time, this person introduced me to some books on ufology, and from the selection of books that he produced for me, I noticed that there were three books that I was immediately interested in. The first book was entitled *'Chariots of the Gods'*, by author Erich von Daniken who believes that the existence of mankind is extraterrestrial in origin, and further states, that the evidence for this can be found in the giant monolithic structures around the world. The second book entitled, *'The Bermuda Triangle'*, by author Charles Berlitz, reveals that the area of ocean near Bermuda is a 'UFO window' and since 1945, when UFO's first became world renowned because of the Roswell incident, is also responsible for the disappearances of over 100 ships and planes, as well as the disappearance of over 1,000 people, who have vanished without trace. The third book, *'Mystery of the Ancients'*, by authors Eric & Craig Umland, builds on the supposition that the Mayans were related to early ancestral spacemen and that in their opinion, this was the staggering saga of Earth's most sinister secret.

The man told me I could have a read of these books any time I wished, and so sometime afterwards, I began reading them and as I read the contents of each book, I began to recognise the familiarities surrounding the UFO phenomenon that had mirrored my own experiences. I also discovered some information about the orange ball of light, which as a young boy playing in the woods at the rear of our house, mentioned in a previous chapter, had convinced me that something strange and unexplainable was going on in our world but until now it seemed that nobody of any political importance was concerned enough to know about it. However, the writers of these books knew something about this startling phenomenon as well as its psychological affects on the people they were writing about and who also clearly knew something about the existence of this phenomenon. From that day onwards I too began to look for further works of this nature in the hope of finding answers and so my quest began.

One most important aspect of these findings was a gradual realisation that this phenomenon had become a worldwide event and I wondered if I would be able to equate these strange instances with those events recorded in the Bible, but for some considerable time after, I was unable to come to any definite conclusions about this possible connection until God revealed to me the meaning behind Genesis chapter 6, where the Lord speaks about his anger at the rising levels of crime in the era prior to the flood. In this chapter He reveals that certain unearthly connections between the 'Sons of God' and the daughters of men, appeared to centre on sexual favours and which, somehow contributed to a great evil catastrophe attributed to the Lord, the Judge of the world, who apparently sent a great flood to destroy all living things in it.

Once I recognised and accepted this particular insight as the beginnings of evidence pointing towards alien existence, I then began to see other Biblical connections throughout both the Old and New Testaments that reinforced my opinions. I began to realise that the Bible was not just a book of spiritual meaning but also a book of historical events containing the past, present, and the future, between its covers. I began to learn something about the kingdom of God and his Word that I believe I could not have learned any other way. It stands to reason, that if there is a God, there must also be a Devil. What is more, if these exist, then there must truly be Angels and if these exist, there must, as the Bible clearly states, also be fallen Angels. Now the Bible is very clear about all this too. If there be fallen Angels, then the only place I could see that they could be fallen to is Earth. This assumption agrees with Enoch who also claims that fallen angels existed here on Earth.

Isaiah the prophet, whom I have quoted in a previous chapter, states that he saw these same 'Fallen Angels' descending to Earth. Was he also quoting Enoch? Like me, Isaiah had a personal experience of the alien enigma and like me he had a copy of the original works of Enoch, which the scribe had written down for his children, who were instructed by him, to give these works of truth to his great grandson Noah who had not yet been born. These works were for preserving the events and people of the past, as well as instructing the people of the 'New World' about the judgement of God.

These works were also the beginnings of the original scriptures and contain references to the second and final judgements yet to befall mankind, as well as precise details of the existence of Angels. However, the Roman Church has sought to eliminate these works from the main body of scriptures and in separating them, have deliberately erased any positive statements within the main body of Biblical text, to omit any precise or clear references to any other works such as those of Enoch.

The reason for this omission is to prevent anyone from learning the truth about the reality of the existence of the Watchers living in our atmosphere and the means of preventing the world from making early discovery of their existence and making contact with them. This type of suppression is something the Roman Church is well practised at, something the Romans are well equipped for, as history shows us.

The answers that I found at that time presented me with an even deeper mystery and I wondered where else to start looking for further corroboration. It was unclear about what I was looking for exactly, when in 1985, I began to experience some new revelations that opened my eyes to the wider issues about the alien phenomenon and how these are related in part to the changes now taking place in the world at large.

What sparked this new direction for me was the news about the end of the cold war era and of Perestroika that begun in the days of the Russian, Mikhail Gorbechev (see chapter fourteen), who was the Soviet Prime Minister at this time. These historical events led up to the most amazing changes regarding the removal of the so-called 'Iron Curtain' and the eventual tearing down of the Berlin wall in 1989. Little did I know then, that a short time spent in Hungary ministering the Gospel, would reveal a prophetic message that would happen in my lifetime? That message was about a revelation given to my father and myself by God during one of our speeches. As we spoke independently to the listeners, we saw that Hungary appeared to be like a bowl that was due to an impression of the mountains and hills roundabout its borders, representing the rim of the bowl. Through this revelation we informed the Hungarians that God was going to set them free and that this work he was doing in their country would eventually overflow the rim of the mountains and spread to other iron curtain countries and the world.

On another occasion, a similar message was given when ministering on the topic "Moses and the fruitful bough" that the freedom that God would give the Hungarians would only occur if they would wholeheartedly put their trust in The Living God and not the powers of men, as well as serve only him and not be afraid. This again was a prophetic message which, when confirmed and added to the previous message, spelled out God's plan for the freedom of Hungary and its believers. These particular prophesy messages came to pass between 1985 and 1989, and Hungary was the first Communist country to tear down its iron curtain fences to let the world in.

Who could have known that this would be possible, except God? Who could have invented Perestroika and used this 'political stone' to tear down communism, except God? Yet despite this connection with major world events, men will still wont to take credit for something that, only God himself did.

When I personally witnessed this happening in 1985, and the subsequent events that followed it over the next five years, I began to see God's word in a newer way and through this means, He showed me things I could never have hoped to understand or know about.

After these events began, the Lord woke me up one night and revealed to me to get a map (but not just any map), an atlas. So I started to look through the maps and atlases I already owned, but could not see what new revelation it was that the Lord was trying to show me in relation to the phenomenon of changes he was bringing about and despairingly I became upset and frustrated at this. However, a few weeks later my wife and I were walking through a local market place where sometimes, there is a bookstall present, selling second-hand books, mostly novels and such like, but on this occasion, the seller had several boxes of interesting books available and I browsed through them.

Among these boxes of books, was an old style *Hammond Atlas*. I picked it up and hurriedly flicked through it, but by now I had become convinced that I may have got it wrong about what God was showing me and so put it back in the box. As I did so, my wife nudged me and said: "I thought you said you were looking for an atlas. That might be what you are looking for!" "I know!" I said, "but I don't think it's that one somehow," but at the same time, I picked up the book for a second look. Then flicking through the pages at the back of the atlas, my eyes fell onto some maps of Israel and the Middle East, when suddenly I saw something of what God was trying to show me and I could not believe my eyes and so I bought the book immediately and a new phase of understanding was opened to me.

God took me back to the book of Daniel through these maps and once again, to the early chapters of Genesis. Here the Lord began showing me his plan for changing the current political structures of this world. He told me, "He was realigning the ways of this world with his word." In other words, He was bringing into effect biblical prophecy at the time that certain prophetical events would now begin to occur from the year, 2001, as this was the period of man's history that it was meant for. However, in order for me to know the future of these events I too would have to undergo some personal changes in my life, which is what the Lord does to someone when he starts working in their lives. (See any of the books of the prophets for examples of these sorts of changes that can come about).

From that time onward, I began to experience a number of dreams and in some of these dreams I walked in strange places and in secret passageways and pathways, some of which exited at unfamiliar mansions or caverns. I could not understand the purpose of these explorations except to know that, again I was being led along some hidden path to enlightenment. This method of initiation appears to be one way that God is able to bring us to a point of faith where the revelation that He gives us must be accompanied by an understanding of the scriptures that he shows us. We can only benefit in our knowledge of God, if what is happening to us is of God. Sometimes it may appear that we are alone and our experiences are not of God. Herein is the need for faith and trust in the Lord. The answers never come straight away and there are lessons that have to be learned first, before we are rewarded or entrusted with the information or revelation that God wishes to impart to us. Sometimes we may never fully understand what God is saying but He will never deviate from His word and if we are unable to glimpse the truth of this, then we have to undergo much more stringent testings.

The secret is to realise that what is taking place during the event, has a purpose that God alone has attached to it. That is what the Lord prefers us to seek out and when we do this, we are ready for the revelation and truth that He desires to impart. In my case, this revelation was concerning disillusionment and world change marked by a tendency towards global warming and increasing acts of violence and lawlessness in a world constantly at war, but that for now, the events regarding Perestroika, has enabled God to cast the stone that has changed the worlds view of empire building and brought into focus a newer destiny for mankind, involving the destruction of Iraq and the climate for the mark of the beast on the European Common Market. The road to Armageddon and judgement day is drawing ever closer and unless these days are 'shortened' there shall no flesh be saved.

"In those days the Lord bade (the Angels)
to summon and testify
to the children of the Earth
concerning their wisdom;
show it unto them; for ye are their guides . . .

that I (God) and My Son will be united
with them for ever in the paths
of righteousness in their lives;
and (in return) ye shall have peace:
rejoice ye children of uprightness,
Amen"

(The Book of Enoch: cv.1; page 150).

CHAPTER THIRTEEN

Disillusionment & World Change

Our modern world is so full of human misery and degradation that it is easy to become extremely disillusioned by everything and everyone around us. Since 1982, nowhere was this so easily apparent than in the churches. All kinds of new doctrines and religious practices were being introduced, such as the community churches, established initially under the auspices of the Church of England and which includes the more recent introductions such as the 'Alpha Course' for example. Eventually, I got used to it being this way because I felt that I personally could not change the things I was both hearing and seeing. The churches now appeared to be practising a form of Christianity that I could no longer recognise or accept as truly scriptural.

It soon became apparent to me that these new spiritually devised systems are nothing short of 'leavened bread' now being metaphorically dished up to the people many of whom were already converted. A true case of the "converted, preaching to the converted!" and in this new form of dogma and worship there is a failure to spot the untruths that seem to be creeping in to these systems. In my opinion this is a revival of the old Roman methodology or a form of Pelagianism subtly being reapplied into mainstream church worship and is aimed at controlling true believers whilst at the same time substituting a spiritual gospel with a moral gospel secretly backed by the government. Could this be the means by which, the masses are controlled and guided into a particular form of religiosity indicated by part of Tolkien's *Fellowship of the Ring,* wherein he cites: the one ring to rule them all, the one ring that finds them, the one ring that brings them all and in the darkness binds them (Tolkien 1981, page 7), when the purpose of Jesus is to set us free from the law of sin and death.

Moreover, this particular form of religious dogma binds up, or 'constipates' believers, and prevents them from individually communing with God to be sustained by the meat of the word of

God in order to survive what lies ahead of us in these troublous times. St. Timothy warns us about these days, but we are only given the milk of the word because the preachers who dish it out, are only capable of serving milk to the people of the church. No wonder congregations are dwindling, and no small wonder why we are fast becoming a Godless society. Could this particular methodology, including rationalism, be the result of their own shallowness and lack of faith in biblical truths and real personal religious experience, or could this simply be the result of insufficient faith in the living God?

Knowing this makes me feel like Bunyan's pilgrim in 'Pilgrims Progress', when he fell into the 'Slough of despond' and seemed unable to pull himself out without help. Although these issues seem to be part of the religious, social and political quagmire caused by the many changes now taking place in our world and the uncertainties of our futures, we must not lose sight of God's Love for us. We must never blame God for our predicaments. However, I keep reminding myself that it is God who is making these changes not only in my personal way of life, but also in the lives of everyone who exists in this world, because He is realigning the way of the world with His word in order to bring to pass prophetical elements of scripture that are intended for this time in the history of man. The purpose of this is that: "He whom the Lord loveth, He chaseneth..." and furthermore, the lord actually requires us to: "...be zealous therefore and repent!" This wondrous word of scripture shows us that we are not infallible, and that the Lord knows the world will drift from time to time and perhaps lose sight of the purposes of God, but He makes it possible for us to return to him, for his love and forgiveness but only true believers within the church, can know this joy.

Often, this is God's way of stripping us of our personal fleshly desires and ways, in order that he may bring us to a place of subjection to himself. Anyone who considers this not to be the way of God cannot truly know Him, whom to know, is eternal life. Neither can they understand the saying that: "He, (JESUS), must bring all things into 'subjection' unto Him, (God the Father). How can they understand this, when the world teaches us to be 'objective', but if we are in Christ, we must become subjective, in order to truly be one with Him. Naturally, we cannot do this of our own selves. It must be and can only ever be, by the Spirit of God, who indwells us, teaching us according to his holy will, at the cost of doing things according to our own fleshly wills, for the ways of the flesh is outside of the kingdom of God. I too, long for, and thirst for, the right ways and the straight, narrow pathway of God.

In 1985, I began to realise the truth of this, that all our efforts are worthless without the stirrings of the Spirit of God within us. During this time also, I began to experience a phase of heightened senses, which I can summarily describe in point of fact, I also had numerous dreams. In these dreams I travelled to strange places. I visited old and ancient buildings, underground places and caverns or stranger still, places that I cannot identify whatsoever. Some places were in total darkness, others in brilliant light. Quite why this should be, I cannot really tell but I realised that Enoch experienced similar events in his dealings with the watchers and in particular, the archangels who took him, and with whom Enoch travelled to numerous locations on Earth and in space, in which, the Archangels showed him all kinds of strange and eerie experiences (Cited in: Charles 1997, pages 39, 44, 47-48). As for me, this type of experience went on for a long time and often when they occurred I was afraid of some of the things I was experiencing. Enoch, on the other hand was a privileged man in the presence of these archangels, because they would reveal the meaning of his visions and experiences directly to him, face to face.

Someone I once shared these dreams with, thought that it sounded like I was having some kind of "out of body experience", but I just did not know. Then one day, I discovered the book of Enoch and realised that he had similar phenomenon occurring in his life too, then gradually my spirit was rekindled and the wellspring that God has placed within me, like rivers of living water, refreshed my soul, praise the name of the Lord and it was here through the book of Enoch that I started to learn what the Lord was about to do in the world. Would I recognise his handiwork? Indeed I did. Enoch was shown many future events that would establish forever God's plan of righteousness and judgement for the people of Earth and this includes the angels as well, as already discussed in the previous chapter.

Perestroika had begun in Russia and little did anyone realise at the time, but this new freedom movement in Russia was about to bring into focus a major world change. God had previously revealed to me that this "Perestroika" was the very means by which he would begin to bring the world into true alignment with his Word.

Perestroika was the stone God himself cast to the feet of the old Babylonian order that had currently persisted in the world until this time. I heard and understood this meaning but many will not. Clearly, (the churches), are not prepared for what God is doing in the world at this time.

I cannot understand how the churches can remain so silent at a time when God does something that they should clearly be able to recognise as only of him. Maybe this is the reason. God is doing something that the Churches do not authorise themselves. So, it cannot be possible for the Churches to see his mighty hand at work. Are these therefore, not like those five foolish virgins that Jesus spoke of, who having run out of 'oil' at a time when the Lord was coming, thought it more important to run to those (Pastors) who sold 'Oil' for gain, as a result, missed what the Lord was doing and when they returned, He (the Lord), did not recognise them? Clearly, they were silent because they could not see God. As he has said: "He hath blinded the eyes of them that see, so that in seeing, they see not."

Perestroika grew from a pebble into a very large stone; this was the changing strategy of the Living God to bring the ways of men into clear alignment with the ways of God. Who among you can foretell this and not give God the glory? It is written: "Great things HE hath done…"

The leaders of this world like to think that they are in control of all we think and say and do, but this is not so, for the Lord God of heaven and Earth, rules in the affairs of the kingdoms of men.

During this period of my life, I began to witness the events of change unfolding. The national and international headlines reported daily on the increased changes that Perestroika was having upon the eastern block countries of Europe.

At the same time as this event was unfolding, Hungary was preparing to tear down its fences and open its gates to the west. This was followed in 1989/1990 by the tearing down of the 'Berlin Wall' that had separated East Germany from West Germany, since world war two. Who could have predicted these events, except the Lord himself? I have no doubt that many will come out of the so-called woodwork, to claim their paralleled predilections, as referring to these events.

No sooner, after the events of Perestroika, the world is again placed in turmoil and confusion when in 1990, Iraq steps onto the world stage with an onslaught on Kuwait. Saddam Hussein seeks to become a religious and political dictator in the Middle East.

Once more, we witness the prophecies of the Bible coming to pass. God, having changed the way the world was going prior to 1985, has now ensured that everyone living today will be concerned about his or her future. Equally more so, by the suddenness of the recent events occurring in Europe and the world. That they would eventually question, 'Is this the beginning of the second Judgement?'

Certain unease was beginning to creep across the globe. The Americans, the British, as well as the French sought to quell this new expression of dictatorship caused by Iraq and their hold on the oil wells in Kuwait. However, Saddam Hussein was being driven by a different cause. All efforts to plead with him were met by fears of a military build up along the northern borders of Israel and Arabia. The dictator of Iraq was now using the situation to promote a *'Holy Jihad'* or 'Holy war' against Israel as an 'ace in the hand' if the west tried to intervene in the Middle East.

Perestroika also opened the way for another major event on the world's stage, when Yugoslavia eventually began to revive old feelings of racial hatred between the Serbians and Bosnians and other ethnic minorities living in that country. For them, Perestroika has meant the withdrawal of Russian troops and a return to their old ways. No sooner said than done, Ethnic Cleansing and holy jihads were springing up everywhere as mankind was thrown back to the dark ages of a now uncertain future for mankind. World peace was now further away than ever before.

The Bible says: "...In the day that we cry 'Peace, peace, peace', then will come sudden destruction." Thus, what we were witnessing at this time was the fact that men, left to their own devises, will only behave in a destructive manner, as they have always done. This is what happens when we omit God from our lives.

From these events and the maps that God had instructed me to get, I was shown the meaning and the timing behind the revelation of the book of Daniel. I stood in a vision of the scriptures, where Daniel had stood and I looked up and saw as Daniel had seen. Standing there, at the banks of the river Ulai, close to the ancient palace of Sushan, Suza, I saw plainly for the first time, the ram that had two horns that stood strangely high on its head, as witnessed by Daniel of old. I saw also, the mighty goat that came from the west and whose feet touched not the ground. I saw the ram move toward the south and toward the north and toward the west, kicking and butting. No one seemed to prevent it. The ram did as it willed and currently this vision remains a true picture of Saddam Hussein and the country of Iraq today, though a little subdued for the moment.

This image of the goat, which has come from the west, has a notable horn between its eyes. This horn is like a semi pyramid-like triangle and carries the inscription *"In et odor Seclorum"* (one world order), and it bore another inscription in the form of the letters "E.F.U.", (European Federal Union). This goat and its horn can be found in any atlas, including the image of the ram, because as He has shown me, God always has a literal and physical mirror image to reflect the spiritual image, as portrayed in his word. God's word is true in every respect.

I stand by this word and all that I have seen, for God is true and faithful to those who believe. On the tenth of August, 1918, at the end of the 'Ottoman Empire', Britain and France were involved in partitioning the Middle East as newly revived conflicts, like that observed in recent times in Yugoslavia, began to surface once more in Israel and the middle east as the Ottomans departed.

The result of this influence, a direct result of the influence of the newly formed "Council of Ten," meant that the boundaries of the Middle East were redrawn. The world atlases would reflect the new scheme of things. Thus the vision of Daniel at Suza was become a reality by the year 1920, when the physical boundaries began to take shape in the real world, the ram was finally born. Nevertheless, the man that becomes the true 'beast' of Daniel's vision is not yet born until 1958.

An opportunity to establish a throne and a lineage followed but a deadly coup masterminded a republican take-over that is the latest sign of world domination in a covert form. Republicanism has the blood of millions on its hands. However, republicanism is not alone in the world of atrocity and the quest for power. This factor is seen in Daniel's goat, which: "came from the west and touched not the ground." The politics of the 'goat', whilst being different in nature, is so strikingly similar to the 'ram', in that it seeks total annihilation of any other beast that may seek to dominate.

Daniel declared the fate of the ram in the scriptures: "The goat cast him down to the ground, and stamped upon him." This remains a true account of recent events in the world today and more especially since the destruction of the world trade centre in New York in September 2001, which has witnessed American outrage on Middle Eastern terrorism, is also said to be the source of this event. That, which Daniel prophesied of old, was spoken for these days in which we now live. The 'ram' is the product of twentieth century politics as is the 'goat' which, in its final two phased form, (goat and horn), is a long-standing creation whose history has been one of continued conflict and suppression of people and nations. The 'goat' has its final reckoning in the twenty-first century as God makes his word come alive in our time.

Fragment of the book of Noah

'And I, Enoch, answered and
said to him' (the one that seeketh truth):
"The Lord will do a new thing on the Earth,
and this too I have already seen in a vision,
and make known to thee
that in the generation of my father Jared,
some of the Angels of heaven
transgress the word of the Lord"

(The Book of Enoch: cvi-cvii.13).

CHAPTER FOURTEEN

Angels of Light

"And your young men shall dream dreams and your old men shall see visions." (Cited in the Book of Joel).

  Perhaps, the most uncanniest aspect of any event affecting change in humans, especially events of a supernatural nature, is the fact that when these occur, it is always without warning. Hundreds of stories are told each year in which people encounter strange experiences that not only bring a sense of fear and dread or confusion to the person experiencing the event, but also inflict a need for change or redirection of individual behaviour. Sometimes, the impact of the event is so great that those who experience them are unable to recognise or interpret any rational understanding for the occurrence, and thus they seek to suppress the events subconsciously, or rationalise it until it becomes meaningless. Nevertheless, they become deeply affected by the strangeness of the event or the images contained within it. This in turn brings a sense of fear, inner denial, anger or contempt, or alternatively, exposes the individual to a higher sense of purpose.
  History is founded on evidence of this nature and great cities have also been built such as the founding of 'Rome' or the more contemporary 'Salt Lake City' in Utah, USA and Washington DC, for example.
  Sometimes, paranormal supernatural events, carry with them possible fraudulent encounters and claims that are so well copied and practised, that it can be hard to determine the true from the false.
  The Bible contains references to both aspects of the phenomenon. For example, the story of Baalam (Cited in: Numbers Ch 22-24). This man is recorded in the bible as some kind of 'wizard' who makes use of several methods for obtaining heavenly knowledge including the ability to obtain through enchantments, the apparent Word of God?

Here is a man who claimed to talk to angels as well as the dead, and who claimed to be able to predict the future, amongst his other famed abilities. In fact, Baalam was exceptionally well known in the ancient Middle Eastern world for his paranormal expertise, that kings would hire him to cast spells or make curses on their enemies.

It is amazing how many people will dabble with occultic matters of this nature, even today. The story of Baalam unfolds with the king of 'Bashan' or ' Og ', commanding the seer to speak words of enchantment against the king's enemies, namely the people of Israel. Baalam was on his way to meet the king of Og upon one of the highest mountains overlooking the land of Israel from whence he would make his predictions and curses, as was his remit for hire. However, even this professional dabbler of the occult had never experienced the reality of the events he was about to encounter on route to Bashan.

The story continues with Baalam walking along a lonely road with his colt or donkey when suddenly the donkey begins to behave unruly and would not go any further along the road. (This behaviour involving animals and pets is something that is well documented in numerous other paranormal and UFO encounters throughout history). Baalam attempted to placate his fore-legged companion but to no avail.

This must have had some impact on the actions of Baalam himself because the Bible indicates that at this point he became disturbed at the animal's reluctance to move forward and this in turn provoked anger in Baalam, who began to violently whip the donkey. The animal found it impossible to move forward and unable to move backwards because of his master's own behaviour towards him.

Suddenly, the animal found the means to converse with Baalam, in which he could also explain the reason for this predicament in the first place. The donkey informed Baalam that a 'shining Angel,' a watcher from heaven, was standing on the road ahead with a flaming sword in his right hand. Then Baalam was struck with fear at the speech of the donkey and filled with dread when suddenly he too could see what the donkey had described to him.

Unlike many paranormal activities we read about, this one is recorded as having a profound sense of purpose. The Angel with the sword was sent to warn the false prophet not to heed the desire of the king of Bashan in cursing the people of Israel, for to do so, would bring a judgement of God upon those perpetrators who would be operating against the will of God.

This event carried with it a warning, as well as a specific command and a set of precise instructions, to which Baalam was ordered to comply. This event also carried a sense of impending doom if the instructions were not adhered to.

Baalam experienced a tremendous change of personality that is referred to later in the story when he finally gets to meet the king of Bashan and is ordered, upon pain of death, to co-operate with the king's plans for Israel.

Baalam clearly could not fulfil the king's desire because of his encounter with the Angel of God and found himself prophesying only good things about Israel. To his own utter amazement, he was speaking things he did not naturally understand and which, occurred to him instantaneously, having his eyes wide open in a miraculous way, not using trances and enchantments as he was so used to doing. How could this be?

Baalam had had an encounter with the true and living God in a way that for him was far in excess of his normal chagrin-like, paranormal activities.

Everyone is entitled to have at least one *'extraordinary'* experience in their lives for which there may be no rational explanation whatsoever, although personally, I am a firm believer that events of this nature, do not occur for nothing.

Our usual failure as humans, is our ability to rationalise everything, and pigeonhole our experiences into all kinds of fleshly, man-made ideas, interpretations or rationalised explanations. In this way, we cleverly detract from the true purpose or nature of the event and because of the existence of this attitude, mankind is effectively denied the revelations or knowledge that such experiences may bring us.

I have already described in previous chapters that mankind's observational skills always prefer the rational so-called scientific explanation of any event beyond the normal everyday experiences of our world. (See chapter one for further explanation of this point).

Both Enoch, and Noah describe early antediluvian paranormal events, including dreams and visions, which they reasonably experienced and which refer specifically to events of their future, namely the 'first judgement' of God upon the world. Furthermore, they receive precise instructions for the salvation of those that would not only listen to them, but also believe them.

Sadly, as in our modern age, hardly anyone believes in anything truly paranormal unless there is money to be made out of it. If that is the case, then it is the product of fraud. However, to ignore any revelation from paranormal experience, in particular, those experiences that carry warnings or instructions, brings with it the detriment of judgement upon unbelieving mankind leading to severe loss of life.

Once again, the Bible is one such literary foundation of truly paranormal experiences that fits my description of the type of future events recorded in its pages, that mankind blatantly refuses to acknowledge, or accept even today. This is especially so because of our rational schools, universities or faculties of Religion, Philosophy, Psychology, Science and medicine, which control the way we think or behave toward anything outside our own worldly interpretations and values.

As always, we only believe in what we ourselves do in that we convince ourselves of all matters relating to life and death through the gods of our own making. Unless we are in control of our world and the events affecting it, nothing that happens beyond our control is deemed real, and therefore cannot be truly possible.

The story of Baalam is one of great interest in the quest for truth with regard to the subject of 'Angels' or 'Alien Beings' visiting our planet. This is because, like all other recorded paranormal events, it contains 'classic encounter material' so common to many modern UFO enigma stories regularly ignored by the mainstream press and denied by government agencies especially, British and American agencies.

The Bible repeatedly describes encounters of 'Paranormal Activity' in which those who experience the surreal nature of these strange encounters, are undoubtedly 'selected' or, to use a biblical expression, 'predestined' to do so, long before the encounter takes place. The Bible states: "Those whom *(God)* did foreknow, He predestined."

Written in the doctrines of the Churches is the *'Doctrine of Predestination'*, so rarely taught these days and which is a vital aspect of Christian belief since the time of the early church fathers. From the very beginning of mankind's history, it is recorded that 'God' has visited and communed with man.

From Adam right up to the present day, God has consistently made himself known to mankind in ways that have been methodical, and life changing. The world may laugh at those who have encountered 'His Presence', it may scorn those who claim differently, but the world cannot run away from the inevitable 'final judgement' waiting to take place although it may be possible to delay it, as demonstrated by the book *'The Bible Code'*.

In 1989, I had another personal experience. I had a further strange dream, possibly the strangest of all the dreams I have experienced so far. Asleep in my bed, I awoke from sleep with a suddenness filled with extreme anxiety at approximately 2.30 am. My eyes wide open, I could still see vividly all the details of what I just experienced whilst asleep. I consciously recall every detail even now - it was so real. In my mind, I am conscious also, that I was in a deep state of sleep, a contradiction of terms here, I know. Then suddenly I hear a noise like that of 'rushing wind' and then a 'Whoosh' sound at which point, I am stood outside a large, wooden, very old style door. Suddenly, I am stood on the other side of this door and I am in a room with a low-beamed ceiling, dimly lit and which I could discern quickly that there were two levels.

At this point, I am stood in the lower level. I look around and all I can see is lots of trestle-like tables and benches like those seen in 'olde worlde inns' and on the tables and the benches as well as on the floor were lots and lots of beer glasses of different shapes and sizes. Some, I observed, were 'half full' and some were 'full' of beer or clearly of various stages of having been drunk from. This knowledge was acquired in split seconds of a moment of time. Furthermore, in that same moment I was equally conscious of a very tall hooded/cloaked being stood to my left. Holding me by the back of my neck he said, in a deep commanding voice, "Drink!" at which point also I suddenly found myself bending down and picking a glass of partial beer dregs, from off the floor; and powerless to resist, I immediately drank as ordered. A second later I am spluttering and spitting and brushing my hands fervently across my face in a frenzy, as the 'beer' I was drinking, became a glass of maggots, which fell on my face the second I tipped the glass to my mouth. In the next second, I heard the sound again of 'rushing wind' followed by a 'whooshing' sound and I am back in my bed asleep.

Suddenly, the realisation that an uncanny event had occurred caused me to wake up immediately. Overcome with fear at what I now realised I had experienced that night, I swung my feet out of bed and sat for a few minutes stunned by the vision and images in my head. Every detail was so real including the taste in my mouth that I decided to go to the bathroom and brush my teeth. Whilst in the bathroom, I washed my face, brushed my teeth, and then rinsed my mouth. As I did so, it was then that I observed a little maggot crawling along the bottom of the sink to my right where I had just spat my mouth rinse. I was shocked! It was then that I realised that this was no ordinary dream or nightmare. It was an event, which carried with it some special meaning.

Determined to find the answer, I consulted a little book I had recently acquired entitled, *'Your Dreams & what they mean'*. Eventually I came to an understanding of what I had experienced that night. God revealed to me in the form of a dream-like encounter, that from this moment on the world would undergo 'Great Changes'.

This message was also to be added together with the message I received from him back in 1985. In this earlier message, God revealed to me that "He was realigning the world with His word, to bring to pass what He has promised" and this was to be signified by the "Grand Cross" alignment of the planets. Now, in 1989, He was about to bring a time of "great change" upon the world such as has never been seen before. Some time after, God also revealed to me, that: "As in the days of Noah so it shall be" in this period before Jesus comes in 'His promised return'. I noted the scriptures concerning these words and discovered so much revelation of what God is doing at this time.

I considered the silence of the churches and marvelled at their apparent ineptitude to realise the signs that God was giving at this time. For God never does anything without revealing it to his witnesses or prophets or disciples or the mouth of two or three witnesses by which, a 'thing' (a truth or event or occasion or revelation), is truly established. I am not alone in the knowledge of these matters. Enoch also described in full, each event that this world has encountered and will encounter, long before it has taken place. Enoch has also recorded these occult ventures in his writings and ensured their survival through Noah unto the present day, when understanding should be given to know 'these things, which shall befall us'.

Jesus also discussed at length in the Gospels the signs and times of the state of the world in which: "all these things shall be fulfilled" (Matthew Ch.24 v 34). These strange, yet awesome encounters I have written about mirror something of the high strangeness encountered by Enoch, and align with the same contextual work of the prophets mentioned in the Bible, whilst at the same time making full use of the meanings behind some of the scriptures themselves. Since the whole affair has been one in which scripture is examined in new light, and revelation gained from these experiences, one can only conclude that the essence of guidance and purpose described in this book is also an act of God. My own realisation that the church's 'lukewarm Christianity' cannot perceive the word of God in true prophetic language due to blindness and lack of understanding, means that God has to find alternative scriptural ways to communicate his plans.

The Angels of God also have their part to play in the unfolding of God's purposes. For this reason, paranormal activity might be part of the methodology chosen to bring about a raising of consciousness, not only in the world at large, but also among God's own people. Who then will hear what the Holy Ghost is saying to the people?

Conversely, Paranormal increase may be the result of a decline in the true ministry of God's Word in that mankind can no longer respond to the word of God and that the Gospel of salvation is no longer preached to the world. Could this also be a sign that the end has come? For Jesus said: "this Gospel shall be preached in all the world and then the end shall come" (Matthew Ch. 24 v 14).

"But in those days
blessed are all they
who accept the words
of wisdom, and understand them,

and observe the paths of the Most High,
and walk in the paths of His righteousness,

and become not godless with the godless;
For they shall be saved`"

(The Book of Enoch: xclx.10; page 142)

CHAPTER FIFTEEN

Further Strange Encounters

It could be said, that the effects involved in the staging of strange phenomenon might require the relationship of a catalyst, in order to motivate the sequence and timing of the particular phenomenon taking place.

This would also imply that a certain set of rules or conditions would need to exist, or be immediately engineered, in order to facilitate the event. Furthermore, this implies that a great deal of intelligence would be required, not only to produce the experience, but also successfully give the event meaning and purpose on the part of the one or more persons involved.

This type of event, described in the Bible with regard to the conversion of Paul for example, (The book of Acts), is the kind of phenomenon often noted as being without warning on the part of those who experience events such as this. What is more, the person experiences the phenomenon against their will such as in the case of alien abduction. So too, is the experience of so-called 'sleep paralysis', in which the victims of such, often describe beings holding them down on their beds and suffocating them whilst doing other activities, said to be of a sexual nature. Incidentally, a connection between alien abduction and sleep paralysis appears to contain similar sexual agendas.

There are also other kinds of reported phenomenon repeatedly occurring throughout the world. These events clearly indicate that something beyond our physical known abilities is going on around us and appears to have some quasi-supernatural or supernatural properties attached to them. Scientists are now beginning to question not only the significance of 'fourth reality beings', but also the possibility of the existence of a 'fifth' dimension in space/time existence, that may contain fifth dimension beings.

The knowledge recently afforded the scientific communities with regard to atomics and physics, especially in the field of 'Quantum Physics', has spawned new revelations of 'worlds within worlds' as being a distinct possibility, much like the ants and humans.

In the world of magic, the apparent supernatural connection is strongly implied and its mentors of the so-called 'black arts', are frequently demonstrated in the public eye.

One such personality regularly featured in newspaper reports, magazine articles and television shows, is 'Uri Geller'. This man claims to have supernatural powers of the mind and regularly bends spoons and stops or starts clocks and watches etc., as part of his phenomenal powers.

On one occasion in 1999, I was listening to Sir David Frost doing a live interview with the practised Mr Geller. He was explaining to the audience how everyone could have this power of the mind and use it.

On listening to his banter, I became incensed at the peculiarity of his dialogue and immediately recognised some alto-biblical references to the 'Chaldean principals' of ancient wisdom magic. Thus in conjunction with his references, I was able to recognise a falsehood.

Carried away with my anger I stood up in the room and pointing my finger at the television, I accused Mr Geller of being a 'false prophet'. Thereafter, I switched off the television and went to bed.

Approximately half an hour later, we heard a low humming sound outside, and above the roof of our bedroom. My daughter, who was already asleep, shouted to us, requesting to know what that strange sound was and where it was coming from. In the next instance, I informed them that I could feel an invisible column or force scanning me slowly, but heavily, down my body, from head to toe like a beam of light that moved back and forth. My family could hear the force of this movement as it moved slowly through the house.

The sound began in the corner of the bedroom and moved diagonally towards the corner of the front exit of the house. This force was so real that the curtains were also moving in time with the scanning of the beam. I shouted out for my family not to panic and I informed them that I was being scanned by an invisible force and that I felt that this was some kind of examination of my being as a direct result of my statement regarding Uri Geller that night. I was aware of many of his claims and in particular those of his UFO encounters.

My family were frightened by this experience and asked me what it was. I told them that it was a UFO hovering over our house because of my statement about Geller.

A few nights later I was awakened from my sleep at around 4.30am to the sound of heavy movement coming from the ceiling above my head. Hard to define in words, but it sounded like the roof was being replaced at speed. I had a brief feeling that I had been taken out of my bed through the roof and then bought back. The noise I heard was the roof being swiftly reconstructed like some clever Chinese puzzle. Strange indeed!

The next day, after examining the garden and the roof for evidence of my experience of the night before, I relayed this event to my family. Later I informed friends and relatives of these experiences.

They could offer no plausible explanation for them. On the other hand I was fully aware of what I had experienced and could find similar experiences within the Bible itself to confirm and justify them.

In the year 2001, I discovered a small paperback book by Lynn Picknett & Clive Prince, titled the *'Stargate Conspiracy'* in which, I learned about their revelation exposing a strange connection with Mr Geller, the CIA, Remote Viewing and UFO's. In their book they mention several personnel from various occupations, such as showmen, entertainers, artists, magicians, congressmen, and the military services as well as the secret services, all of which appear heavily involved in some way with the 'secret world order conspiracy', as suggested by these authors.

This type of information, which other famous writers have discussed openly and in much detail in their respective individual works, serves to confirm that we are bordering on the 'apocalyptic age' as we witness the many changes being affected in the world at this time. In addition, these works confirm, in a roundabout way, the revelations of Enoch and the Bible, (even if that is not the various authors' particular intentions).

This is especially so, with the many authors' regard to the biblical 'endtimes of the World', the so-called 'Last Days'. The constructive elements and the well-researched methodology of each independent work carried out by these authors, clearly lends its own conclusions to that of their many readers.

Most of the references used by the authors are the same as used by professional clergymen, doctors of psychology and religion, ministers and evangelists, all over the world. On the other hand, this particular aspect of the question of the events surrounding the concept of the 'Last Days' is also freely understood and politicised by a number of 'anti-groups' within modern society.

These groups will also make great use of the same, or similar references quoted in the Bible and other relevant sources, to define their various, and unscrupulous, political agendas, based on society's fear and insecurities with regard to the future.

Nevertheless, it is certain that something paranormal is taking place in our modern world that has its roots in ancient writings from a variety of historical backgrounds. This paranormal activity has a connection with the first days or early period of mankind and the first judgement upon mankind, and the last days or final judgement of mankind discussed within this chapter.

Once again, the references to paranormal activity is linked, in part at least, to the sightings of UFO's and alien abduction as well as the many strange animal mutilation stories that have also taken place from around the world since 1947.

The American and British governments have created a wall of silence over these and many other paranormal stories not listed in this work. Nevertheless, it has also been suggested, by numerous authors on these subjects, that these governments have been in contact with alien beings and that they have learned about the aliens' propulsion systems and their methods of flight. These same governments are said to have secretly back-engineered these alien flight systems to produce the 'common black project technology' increasingly being witnessed in the skies today. When will the governments of this world come clean and tell the people of the world the whole truth about the many thousands of reported events of UFO's and other related matter witnessed throughout the globe? When it is too late to change things, no doubt? Perhaps, this is the final cause behind the events leading up to the resulting second judgement of mankind?

It is equally strange, that the original causes of alien involvement, led to the primary fall of Adam and Eve, which was later followed up by a second major close encounter of the third kind, when alien beings *en masse,* descended to Earth and began living alongside mankind in the days of Jared. The book of Enoch confirms the facts concerning these events.

It is also strange, that in those days the very same kind of reported events occurred at a time when the expectancy of man was geared towards the concept of the future of mankind. In those days too, there was regard to major global changes, which led to the first judgement in the days of Noah, as predicted by Enoch.

It is this same secret knowledge, which Jesus quotes, when he says in the gospels that: "As in the days of Noah, so shall it be in the days when the Son of Man cometh", (Matthew Ch.24 v 37).

The multitudes of UFO sightings reported throughout the world today appear to mirror the events recorded and prophesied about in the Bible and the book of Enoch. Can we ignore the evidence rapidly occurring in our time?

Are these alien beings really angels of God? If so, how can we be certain that these apparent 'beings of light' are not actually 'beings of darkness'?

The Bible gives us two distinct aspects of God's realm, namely, one aspect of Darkness and the other of Light. In the subject of Angels, the Bible indicates that there are two distinct categories within the realm of Angels. For example: 'Fallen Angels' - Angels of the dark and 'Holy Angels' - Angels of the light.

In the book of Job, we discover that an intergalactic meeting had apparently been convened in which the 'Sons of God' - 'Angels of Light', came to present themselves before the Lord (Job 1 v 6-12). During the proceedings another being named Satan, also came and presented himself at the heavenly meeting place. At this meeting, it appears that he disrupted the proceedings, whereupon the Lord turns to Satan, as if surprised at this intrusion, and questions him of his whereabouts. Satan replies that he has been busy going back and forth to planet Earth and 'walking up and down in it'. It appears that the main reason for Satan's gatecrashing of the intergalactic convention was his concern about the apparent uprightness and behaviour of the Earthman called Job. This situation is repeated on another occasion when it appears that a second conference involving 'the Sons of God' was convened and Satan interrupted this meeting in exactly the same manner as the earlier proceedings. Again, the purpose of this intrusion was to complain about the Earthman called Job, (Job Ch. 2 v 1-7).

Hundreds of years later the book of Luke tells us that Jesus, having sent his disciples to heal the sick and cast out demons, suddenly exclaims that he saw Satan as lightening fall from Heaven. His disciples could not understand what it was he was saying to them or even why he said it but Jesus was quoting from the book of Isaiah in which the ancient prophet was questioning the purposes of Satan in his destruction of the Earth through teaching men violence.

"How art thou fallen from Heaven O' Lucifer, Son of the morning! For you have said, I will ascend above the heights of the clouds like the most high God. I will exalt my throne above the stars of God and sit in the mount of the congregation, (meeting place or galactic conference), in the sides of the north" (Isaiah Ch. 14 v 12).

These statements appear to conjure up a picture of an alien presence evolving around some kind of intergalactic mutiny. From these excerpts, it appears that the Earth and humans are the subject of some jealous rivalry between the Sons of God and a group of beings, whom Enoch refers to in his book as, 'the Satans'. Incidentally, Enoch informs us that violence must increase in the Earth before a resolution of judgement can be made. Jesus warns his disciples that the purpose of the devil (another name for Lucifer) is: "to steal, to kill, and to destroy", (John Ch.10 v 10). If these issues are correct, and the ancient records are to be believed, then it appears that a threatening 'alien presence' has continuously been monitoring the Earth and in particular, the progress of humans.

In fact, when we add up the comments referred to above, it appears that this alien presence has been instrumental in the original causes for war and dissension among the nations throughout history, according to Enoch. The weapons of destruction, and the power to use them, the seduction aspects of mankind initially taught to Eve, the hedonistic principles passed onto Adam, the greed and self-interests of one nation over others, its individuals and societies, have all been introduced to us by aliens in the days of Jared.

These abilities and skills are genetically and socially implanted in us so that we pass them on successfully without fail, from generation to generation until we eventually reach a point in our existence where we are capable of mass destruction. This is what alien contact has been about. A conflict of alien interest between two major groups namely, the sons of God, The Angels of Light and the destructively Jealous, Sons of Darkness, and The Angels of darkness.

The truth has now been told, and it is time to wake up and smell the coffee. Enoch, the Bible and other ancient writings inform us that the only solution to saving this planet from such dastardly influences is for us to take up the cause of righteousness and to walk uprightly before God. Therefore, repent of all our sinful and unbelieving ways, change our hearts and not our minds because, the penalty for not accepting the truth or for not believing the word of God, is that a day of final judgement will surely come upon us. As for the aliens, you need to make certain as to their existence and their purposes for abducting humans, because if it transpires that these beings are truly 'Angels of Light, or Angels of Darkness', then the world really is in trouble. The judgement of God must exist, as an extreme possibility. If alien existence and angels turn out to be one and the same intelligent sentient beings that I believe they are, then what chance is there for the unbelieving human race to save themselves? The only option for mankind is to utilize repentance on a worldwide scale, changing your hearts, not your minds, and seek the salvation of God whilst He still hears us.

So then, what does God's Salvation actually mean for us? "God is love" (cited in The Bible, 1 John ch.4 v 8 & 16), and according to one writer, "the love of God" is considered to be "the most comprehensive and sublime of all Biblical affirmations about the nature of God" (cited in: Blanchard, 1975 page 47). "It is not that God possesses love, as one of his qualities etc., but that His very essence is love. God is love, and love governs His every activity".

Creation was an act of love, (Cited in: The Bible, Revelation ch.4 v 11). The long-suffering nature of God and the numerous opportunities that He has given man (known as grace), in encouraging mankind to repent of his behaviours, is also an act of God's love for us (Cited in: The Bible, Titus ch.2 v 11). The Bible declares that: "God so loved the world, that He gave his only begotten Son (JESUS), that whosoever believes in JESUS shall not perish, but have everlasting life". For God sent not His Son into the world to condemn the world; but that the world through Him might be saved".

The Bible also says: "that men love darkness rather than light because their deeds are only evil, continuously, but, he that doeth truth, cometh to the light, willingly accepting the love of God", (Cited in: The Bible, Gospel of John ch.3 v 14-21). Now, I say to you in the words of Jesus: "if I have told you of Earthly things, and you believe me not, how shall you believe the heavenly things I have spoken of?" (Cited in: The Gospel of John ch.3 v 12). Are Aliens and Angels one and the same existence, and are these beings 'Angels of light or Angels of darkness?' You alone must decide the answer.

Bibliography

BAUVAL, Robert & GILBERT, Adrian: *'The Orion Mystery': Unlocking The Secrets of the Pyramids*, 1994, William Heinemann, London.

BERLITZ, Charles: *'The Bermuda Triangle': The Saga of Unexplained Disappearances*, 1975, Granada Publishing, ST Albans, Herts.

BERLITZ, Charles & MOORE, William: *'The Philadelphia Experiment': The True Story Behind Project Invisibility,* 1980, Granada Publishing, St Albans, Herts.

BLANCHARD, John: *'Right with God': A straightforward book to help those searching for personal faith in God*, 1971, The Banner of truth trust, Edinburgh, Scotland.

BRUNNI, Georgina: *'You Can't Tell The People': The definitive account of the Rendlesham Forest UFO Mystery*, 2001, Pan Books, London

CHARLES, R. H., D Lit., D.D. (1853 - 1937): *'The Book of Enoch': 1917, In a number of early document translations*, Oxford University Press, 25th impression 1997, SPCK, London

DANIKEN, Erich von: *'According to the Evidence': Proof of man's extraterrestrial origins*, 1998, Corgi Press, London.

GILBERT, Adrian & COTTERELL Maurice M.: *'The Mayan Prophecies': Unlocking the secrets of a lost civilization*, 1995, Element Books, Shaftsbury, Dorset.

GOOD, Timothy: *'Unearthly Disclosure': Conflicting Interests in the Control of Extraterrestrial Intelligence*, 2000, Century Books, Random house, London.

GRANT, Jeffrey R.: *'The Handwriting of God': Sacred Mysteries of The Bible*, 1997, Frontier Research Publications Inc., USA.

HAMMOND'S: 'World Atlas - *Classics Edition': An Encyclopaedic Atlas of The World with the Latest and most authentic Geographical & Statistical Information in Maps, Words and Pictures*, 1961, C. S. Hammond & Co., USA.

OVASON, David: *'The Secret Zodiac of Washington DC': Was the City of Stars Planned by Masons?* 1999, Century Arrow Books, London.

POPE, Nick: *'The Uninvited': An expose of the alien abduction phenomenon*, 1997, Simon & Schuster, Viacom, London.

SELLIER, Charles E.: *'UFO': Fact or Fiction - New evidence challenging our assumptions and requiring us to ask questions about the phenomenon,* 1998 Contemporary Books, Chicago, Illinois, USA.

TEMPLE, Robert: *'The Sirius Mystery': Scientific Evidence of Alien contact 5000 years ago.* Revised Ed., 1998, Century Random House UK, London.

TIMES, The: *'Atlas of The Bible': Ed. (By James B. Pritchard),* 1987 Times Books, Harper Collins, London.

WILSON, Colin: *'Alien Dawn': An investigation into the contact experience*, 1998 Virgin Publishing, London.

UMLAND, Eric & Craig: *'Mystery of The Ancients': Early Spaceman & The Mayans - The staggering saga of Earth's most sinister secret*, 1976, Granada Publishing, St Albans, Herts.